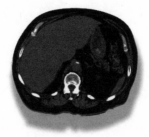

The Shadow Factory

ISBN 978-0-930829-65-0

Lumen Books, SITES Books, and Helen Lane Editions are imprints of
Lumen, Inc., a non-profit, tax-exempt corporation based in Santa Fe, NM
and specializing in literary works, literary translations, and architecture as
well as digital technologies.

Lumen, Inc.
40 Camino Cielo
Santa Fe, NM 87506
www.lumenbooks.org
Printed in the United States of America by Thomson-Shore, Inc.
Design: Dennis Dollens
Distributed by Consortium Book Sales and Distribution
11045 Westgate Drive
St. Paul, MN 5514
www.cbsd.com
1-800-283-3572

The Shadow Factory

Paul West

Lumen Books

BOOKS BY PAUL WEST

FICTION
The Immensity of the Here and Now
Cheops
The Shadow Factory
O.K.—The Corral, The Earps, and Doc Holliday
A Fifth of November
The Dry Danube: A Hitler Forgery
Life with Swan
Terrestrials
Sporting with Amaryllis
The Tent of Orange Mist
Love's Mansion
The Women of Whitechapel and Jack the Ripper
Lord Byron's Doctor
The Place in Flowers Where Pollen Rests
The Universe, and Other Fictions
Rat Man of Paris
The Very Rich Hours of Count von Staufenberg
Gala
Colonel Mint
Caliban's Filibuster
Bela Lugosi's White Christmas
I'm Expecting to Live Quite Soon
Alley Jaggers
Tenement of Clay

POETRY
Tea with Osiris
The Snow Leopard
The Spellbound Horses

NONFICTION
Oxford Days
The Secret Lives of Words
Master Class
My Mother's Music
A Stroke of Genius
Sheer Fiction—Volumes I, II, III, IV
Portable People
Out of My Depths: A Swimmer in the Universe
Words for a Deaf Daughter
I, Said the Sparrow
The Wine of Absurdity
The Modern Novel
Byron and the Spoiler's Art
James Ensor

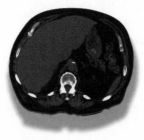

The Shadow Factory

Foreword

One day in June of 2003, Paul lay in a hospital room in Ithaca, NY, watching the sun's hallelujahs beyond the sealed window, and aching to go home. He'd already been there for three weeks with a kidney infection that became systemic, one of those rootin'-tootin' staph bugs older than sharks or gingko trees, and I'd camped out with him, lest he trip over several leashes and lines dripping fluids into or out of him. Struggling from bed, he made his way to the bathroom. The next morning he would be heading home at last.

A few moments later he walked out of the bathroom and stood at the foot of the bed, eyes glazed, his face like fallen ice. Paul had had a massive stroke, one tailored to his own private hell. The author of over fifty stylishly-written books, a master of English prose with one of the largest working vocabularies, a man whose life revolves around words, he had suffered brain damage to the key language areas of his brain and could no longer process language in any form. Global aphasia, it's called, the curse of a perpetual tip-of-the-tongue memory hunt. He understood little of what people said, and all he could utter was the syllable *mem*. Nothing more.

Many doctors, tests, and frantic days followed, and his prognosis was grim. The brain cells were dead in Broca's and some of Wernicke's area, he could no longer swallow food without choking, and it was a left-hemisphere stroke. I'd just published a poetics of the brain, and I knew that the left hemisphere processes positive feelings, the right negative ones; unopposed, the remaining right hemisphere could spark dark angry emotions for the rest of his life.

But Paul had a couple of important traits going for him. Because he had word-smithed for seven decades, he had forged thickets of more brain connections for language than most people. Also, he could be diabolically determined.

After three weeks in the hospital's rehab unit, he was able one day to say proudly: "I speak good coffee," but little more. Still, it was a complete sentence. I took him home, hired speech therapists, who, alas, weren't able to help him move beyond simple utterances. Whenever he spoke, the wrong names for things tumbled out. Aphasia is, above all, a sorting disorder. And, with short-term memory clobbered, by the time he got to the second half of a sentence he had forgotten the first half.

"You know, dear," I said to him one day, about two months after the stroke, when he was feeling mighty low, "maybe you want to write the first aphasic memoir." He smiled broadly, said: "Good idea! *Mem, mem, mem.*" And so he began dictating, sometimes with mountain-moving effort, and others sailing along at a good clip, an account of what he'd just gone through, from the horse's mouth, what the mental world of aphasia felt and looked like. Writing the book was the best speech therapy anyone could have prescribed. For three exhausting hours each day, he forced his brain to recruit cells, build new connections, find the right sounds to go with words, and piece together whole sentences. Going over the text with him the next day helped refine his thoughts and showed him some of aphasia's fingerprints in the prose.

Now, three years later, he has just finished writing a new novel, one with Westian characters and themes. During a three-hour window of heightened fluency in the middle of the day, he can write in longhand, make phone calls, lunch with friends. He has reloomed vibrant carpets of vocabulary, and happily, despite the left hemisphere stroke, he seems happier than before, and I think his life feels richer in a score of ways.

What follows is *The Shadow Factory*, the aphasic memoir Paul dictated with such struggle and resolve, "forcing language back on itself." In it, he recalls life in the early days after his stroke, what he felt and thought, and explores some of the all-too-real tricks the mind plays to save itself from the tomb of lost words.

Diane Ackerman
Ithaca, NY, November 2007

Preface

What follows is an account of two illnesses, the first following hard on the heels of the second. The first invoked an expertly done procedure, allowing me an encounter with the anesthetic Versed, culminating in a shattering explosion of kidney stones that I did not hear. The second, on the eve of my return home from the hospital, was a stroke, which, among other things, deprived me of speech for months and rendered my right arm useless.

Looking back on these untoward happenings, I recognize that sometimes my memories of infected kidney got into and fed my recollections of long months of stroke, and these benign memories entered into the deliriously piercing altitudes of my aphasia. I decided, on recovery, to let sleeping dogs lie where they fell, and this accounts for some of the mixes in presentation.

Half the time, I did not know where I was and, over at least six months, some of my most treasured moments came from I know not where. I only know they were in me, and to be ecstatically treasured, as they still are. T. S. Eliot's "garlic and sapphires in the mud clot the bedded axle tree," far insaner than my first attempt at language: "I talk good coffee." I had achieved language, at last, revived from my months of surveying the world when, I, the literary wonder, was more wordless than a child.

I owe forests of people, more patient than

I, thanks for seeing me through this bitter interim, from which I still have not recovered quite, either stammering or going dumb when I should be doing neither. Such motions of the mouth we call a reversal to type: we try to imagine people less fortunate than ourselves. There but for the grace of God, go I . . .

My steadfast friend, Chris Furst, stayed with me in the trenches of the first drafts and has remained my friend throughout, on a diet of egg salad sandwiches.

My largest debt is to that distinguished poet, philosopher, and woman of letters, Diane Ackerman, who has seen me through many horrors, none worse than this most recent one. Without the providential fortitude of her ministrations I surely would not have survived this far.

To the sympathetic restoration of all and sundry, minus one or two beleaguered, unwanted souls—one a publisher and a few the bedmakers of no great skill—I owe more than I can say even in this knotted labyrinth of a treatise, warts and all. And to have malingered semiconscious through the best of their endeavors is the cruelest cut of all. I hope that, since then, I have put in what I am tempted to call this book (and still may) an appearance of *normality*. Though in truth, any semblance of normality in this aphasiac tale would bring me suspiciously close to my favored realm of fiction.

The attentive reader (or even the inattentive one) will notice run-on sentences, feats of repetition, instances of not getting quite the right word. This is a quite deliberate attempt to mimic the disordered state of my mind in its disheveled post-stroke condition. I remember those jumbled thoughts only too well and remain torn between leaving them in or taking them out: sentimentality triumphant or the letter which kills. In the end I have hedged, favoring both on different occasions, sometimes actually deleting the totally obscure as meaningless. Such the behavior of the mind in extremis, such the gaffes.

Paul West
Ithaca, NY, November 2007

To all of these, my gratitude for seeing me through:

Diane Ackerman,
Dr. Ann Costello,
Dr. John Costello,
Whitney Chadwick,
Ronald Christ,
Elizabeth Butler,
Thomas Eisner,
Chris Furst,
Elaine Markson,
Lucy Garrison,
Irving Malin,
James McConkey,
Dr. Andrew Morpurgo,
Bradford Morrow,
Steve Poleskie,
Jeanne Mackin,
Dr. Sanjeev Vohra,
Robert Wilson,
and several more.

1

The bright wind of morning returned Dr. Sanjeev
Vohra from below in a flash. For a patient who
waited impatiently, for as much as an hour or two,
while the circuitry of Earth made a burrowing sound,
I wanted not at all for time. "There is no pain so
there is no poison." I felt privileged to assist in his
mystery, although the experience seemed much as
before. He who was monarch of all he surveyed was
the archduke and master of us all. First, he showed
me a sonogram with a brown, centrally located ball
that in some ways might have been a fragment of
Mars but plainly was not, as an excited brain raced
on to prove. I was myself caught between affection
for Mars and his balanced presentation.

"This is you," he said briskly, picking up
my unvoiced admiration for the red planet. "This
is you with the red planet, with a bit knocked off.
To go further will require a good deal more. This
had already happened while you were asleep."
I was staggered. How could such telemetric
mellifluousness assault the majesty of time and
space, while giving me not a moment's pause for
five seconds' thought? Instead of responding to his
array of subject matter, as was only prudent and
polite to do, I staggered off into a subject of my
own that was humble to his cosmic endeavors as
mouse is to mountain. It consisted of work long
planned concerning Osiris and his fate among the
rival Egyptians, one of whom, Seth, planned to cut

him into fourteen pieces, just the admirable size for a sonnet. Dr. Vohra blazed on, caught up in his own profundity, stretching the discussion out to a meditation on tungsten and the theory of glass. I tried again to deflect his attention, but it was no use. He was off on his own trajectory to a destination unknown to man. It was safer to let him go ahead and exhaust the gravitas of his theme. He was resuming anyway, coming down to earth with proof that he'd been listening all the time to my doldrums.

Instead, he now proposed the shocking truth about the Foley catheter with which he'd planned— he'd already done it once—to invade my body again with bloody stagnant bags affixed to my feet, a white alarm cord clipped to my upper body to nix my vain hope of plotting an escape. My disappearing act remained in Limbo for the time being. Who knows what fiendish, although delightful tricks would be planned for me in the future?

Vohra was racing ahead as if fired by his own inspiration and, for all I know, would touch down on Jupiter real soon. I could hardly manage to choose between the man's mania and his vivid mind. It was not a matter of choosing either of them but finding some third sum that could bring the world together without breaking either.

At his most humble now, he made arrangements to see me the same evening and told me to get a good meal and not too much milk. As the parting shot, he relayed to me the subject that had been paralyzing his mind for hours, saying, "Your ideas about Osiris will bear much fruit, I can see it now. Just be careful to separate the tungsten from the uric acid." He was gone and I had the distinct impression that I was assisting in the presence of a fakir. The man's presence seemed both magical and commonplace at once. I later realized that the next few weeks would involve me with him much more intimately and teach me more about him than any fakir knows. His shadow was still present though absent, and his worldly being was for a time squandered. I was left to contemplate charms of the Foley bloodbath along with the quart of milk I had summoned up from the cafeteria.

Osiris, my thoughts returned to Osiris and the presence of an almost forgotten object, the oxygen pipe left in my nose ever since the operation began. I sailed out into a partly unknown sea with tungsten, Osiris, the bloody bag, and, not least, Sanjeev, my thoughts illumined by a phantom bag, Sanjeev; my thoughts illumined by the light of an operation that was his and his alone, my fixation on an operation that was something and nothing all at once, how ever long it lasted, and likely to remain so.

II

I never thought that going to the hospital would be such a gracious experience, not with all the fancy pageantry associated with it. In fact, I fancied how anyone vouchsafed such a delightful experience would come away refreshed as if for a thousand lifetimes. There will be white samite on the balconies, purple balustrades on the eves. "False starts." Handsome doctors would be only too glad to donate the wisdom of a lifetime's sciences, and deep in radioactive labs there would be doctors waiting to give you the benefit. And the nurses, of course, freely donate the bounties of a lifetime of mothering. Were such an experience denied anyone of rational mind, they would be heard protesting against their fate in the backwaters of the universe.

I had come prepared for work and work I did, having prepared to toil on Harper & Row's edition of J. M. Coetzee's presentation of my novel, *The Very Rich Hours of Count von Stauffenberg,* as well as a long story about the three Oxford martyrs condemned to the fire in 1556.

In breezed Dr. Vohra again, explaining the delights of a chemical that induces instant sleep. He crowed and obviously delighted the faces of the senior people around him. "It would be as a dream coined by the Arabian Nights, even if only memory of our Horiri plumbed from the depths of the Pacific Ocean. I would even go so far as to recommend it myself."

I was stunned by his felicity with English and the berserk-seeming plumminess of his miracle Indian accent. Besides, he was getting me fresh in the prime of a morning, not, as usual, later in the heat and torpor of afternoon. I agreed even before the words left my mouth. I looked forward to this great experience of an even greater man and even to his recital of the day's events to his children.

Without so much as a murmur the hypnotic Versed passed in and out of my system and I knew no more. When I woke I felt nothing so much as a biting compulsion to take a pee, which the nurse's aide told me was illusory, and all else was a memory of this far-from-shy operator who could supervise an operation he called a "procedure" without pain. When I, a few minutes later, would meet Diane in the waiting room, I was all smiles and gave ample evidence of having been exposed to a great experience. "What are you smiling about?" "I don't know, except the absence of being absent. He gives me such a warm nudgy feeling. I wonder what he tells the doctors who follow him later in the day." Diane made a gesture of gratified comprehension and seemed happy to have her man back in the days of a thousand glories. She had come to meet him on the white road to paradise.

The storm that followed this idyll came right away when I realized that some ferocious apparatus had been attached to my penis, stretching, as I fondly imagined, at least a quarter of my leg, producing a series of howls, asking who or what conspired against me thus. It could not have been my Indian friend of the shining eyes and literate conversation, but I hated him from the very first moment of nodule transmission.

"What's wrong?" asked Diane. "Something's wrong with my balls. They feel as if they've been caught on a stretcher and tugged out to maximum length." I learned later that this devilish appliance was designed by a man called Foley who should be stoned in hell for false contribution. One day later, Vohra freed me of this incubus to science without explaining what he thought it was for and thus exposed me to the phantom tricks of a nurse's aide who, without warning, ripped off the full length of the Foley in one motion, causing me to jackknife upward with a yell.

In explanation she shamefacedly said, "They always do it that way. It makes the pain less intense." I nursed a sore penis for about an hour and then felt freed enough to go to the next room to take a pee. Whatever happened to me next would have no doubt the same characteristics: on the one hand the same subliminal gratification that Vohra spoke of; on the other, the same titanic gullibility that the presumed designer of the Foley had in mind. Never again, though, would I be deceived into thinking the Foley machine would not be called upon to my less than delight. I half wanted to trust Vohra and his conniption-fit English, welcoming a certain renegade in intelligence work, but this author wanted to ram their impolitic device down their throats and challenge them to a game of honest cricket.

     The day would soon approach when I was up for my second exposure to the war machine; it was in fact only six days away. Before that there was a roundtable discussion of the pros and cons. When we eventually sorted out that Vohra would perform, as before, in the freshets of early morning, it was with me looking forward and half back to the delightful stations of my unique history.

III

Vohra's style was neither ungainly nor ostentatious but was rather portly. He suggested mental motions without encouraging us too far and seemed always to keep something in reserve for the errors of outrageous fortune such as myself. He usually visited me in the evening hours when he seemed slightly low-key and certainly more subdued, finally bidding me farewell in an elevated upper-class way that reminded me of his days in India, and prune buns.

It was a slow go of it, although rather pleasant. I had, as I discovered, time to take my time, which in other words meant time to linger over those tall glasses of milk.

So, too, with a rosy-faced, unintimidated provider of low-grade athletic equipment who barged into my curtain. Was I dreaming or not when I provided my obscure scenario, a mellow mood for even such a drastic implement as the Foley, from whom I gleaned a warmer mood? Or was I just dreaming some account of Vohra's own sentimental vogue? It was not his style to indulge in rigmarole of this kind, but one would occasionally snap him digging into the old Indian myth game. I tried to follow him in this, knowing that he was older in the game than I and that I might pick up some useful tips.

There were semibeautiful girls who, as I discovered, could not make beds. Two, especially. One who rigged all the bed linens to the bottom of the bed and left them there or to the tender mercies of some yet unidentified observer, the other a sallow lass who shifted all the bed linens to the top and departed, saying, "Here's to the genius who could make a better job of this than I!" Such creatures are bound to infest the mild pastures of any common dairy farm, but you do not expect two of them in the same dairy.

Further afield, various individuals disported themselves whom I now had time to witness, from the chubby-cheeked loner who with uncurious sleight of hand punched in the schedule of the day, sometime between 4 and 6 o'clock a.m., and left it foaming.

It seemed to me that when a shift announces itself, you should feel a shove. You should feel a shudder or a ripple that threatens not to leave you alone. Always I sent my mind racing or lazing back to Dr. Vohra, for whom I was forming undeniable affection, even with all the flunkydom attached to his Foley. He was my guide in this, counseling me each evening to get some nourishing instead of my liturgical drink of milk. I wasted his advice, shoving nibbled portions of salmon under the tongue quilting with half-digested marzipan.

IV

The most cynical of you know the pleasure of
working for a good time so that the things that are
going well are finished and the force that drives you
still leaves you something to do: when to freshen
the windowpanes or deadhead plants. I myself, on
a temperate spring day, felt the impulse to go even
further and devote myself to sweeping the pool
and then, if time permitted, doing the garage floor.
This would hold me in good aroma for the return of
Diane, who was away on the Coast. I began with the
pool and remarked how little water there was to be
swept up, so I soon began to transfer my attentions
to the garage floor, which had not been cleaned
in twenty years. I began with sweeping trash from
the bases of the floor towards the faint slope of the
driveway. This would exercise my muscles and get
me in good with the people who ran things. I noticed
a faint friction as I moved my body—dismissed it as a
natural secretion of physical movement. It persisted,
however, until by the end of my sweeping it had
assumed the form of a full-blown attack of nerves.
I thereupon desisted and went indoors, wondering
what on earth I had done to offend myself thus.
By the next night my sore back had become a full-
blown attack of something or other and I hurried to
the Convenient Care center to ask what they thought.
    One hour later I had been equipped with
painkillers and the antibiotic Ciprofloxacin, which I
should not have received, and had my lungs x-rayed

and abdomen examined. With one pleasant result that by the time I got home I was feeling no pain.

It was on the northern coast of California that Diane received the news of something untoward happening to me in Ithaca, and she at once changed reservations and took the red eye to be by my side the next morning. When she got back she found me in moderate health, being fed the Cipro and a painkilling drug that appeared to be going down well enough. "You seem to be more than a dying man," she said with her customary wit, and I hung my head in shame after dragging her 3000 miles or more to a nonevent. Nonetheless, she watched me carefully all day, peppering me with questions. I felt all right, I told her, though I had a pain, infinitely subdued, in the neighborhood of my right rib, the fruits of sweeping down the pool and the garage. "It will go away, it's not much of a pain anyway."

But I could see from her face that she doubted my qualifications to appraise my condition. I was well comforted with the painkiller, and she became even more suspicious: "How do you feel without painkillers?" And we at once began an attack on that front. In an hour I was wincing with pain; I was off my food, and clearly something was wrong beyond any thought of Shakespearean chimney sweep going to battle. It was like a temperate acid being ladled across my frame. Now tolerable, now excruciating.

That night, after Diane had gone to bed at her usual 10 p.m., I developed shivering fits and felt dizzy. When I transferred to bed, where I never got a wink of sleep, the pain became more intense, until I began to shake from head to foot. After half an hour of this, I woke Diane and said something was *wrong*. With admirable patience, she saw I had a temperature of 101.3 and located our own doctor, Dr. Ann, as we call her, who arranged for my immediate care at the hospital and said she would be there later on.

On arrival, I was impressed by the speed with which I was triaged and bundled into a comfortable-smelling room with nurses and two aides who proceeded to pummel me from all directions to see if I felt any pain. The only painful part was the rib, which at this point had become agonizing. Apart from that I felt not so bad and even thought what a fraud I was to be in that place of mercy, with what I still believed was a pulled sinew in my gut.

The atmosphere got much graver when a Dr. Allen appeared, whispering something to Dr. Ann. Soon I was informed that I had urine seeping through the kidneys into the body cavity and I must be operated on with no delay. This was a blow after all my romantic courtesies to the pain in my side. There was one other authority who Dr. Ann wished to consult, and he arrived, breathing heavily, with a grave look. He examined me forthwith, and then, after a brief reference to my condition and the need for an operation, queried me with the utmost tact. When Dr. Ann joined the party, which numbered five or six, they followed me upstairs, and thus began one of the strangest intervals in my life, which hung between what I fancied was a gusher of blood and what I hoped would be a mere by-blow.

My brain seemed to dance in dalliance with Dr. Vohra, and my blood felt shuttled one way and the other, which made no sense at all. In fact, though I made sociable noises to Diane and other people when I came around, I remember nothing of the procedure at all, or of my waking up, or of my going to sleep. In my delirium I talked to people whom I could not see, childhood friends and family, that even now, months later, I find no difficulty in placing among the toys of my childhood.

Under other conditions the hospital might have seemed a nice and commodious place to be but not now, as burly employees shifted me around and wheeled me into the emergency ward. The strange thing was that now I didn't feel so bad: with the assist from the painkiller the pain had subdued, and I was able to talk companionably with a couple of nurses. I was even thinking they would soon determine the culprit. I would be back among the foxgloves and irises before I knew it and my name be mired in history forevermore.

Business picked up, however, when a surplus of doctors arrived. Dr. Allen immediately got into the huddle and would pay me off or pay me out. The routine medical examinations had been already done. What was left was secret to me until Dr. Ann arrived with a grave face and said, "You have blood pouring into your urine and your temperature is

101.3. This is serious." Well, I didn't feel so bad and was bracing myself for the act of eviction, so I gave her an amused look and said, "Really? I don't feel so bad." "In fact so bad," she said, "that when the next attack comes around you'll be pleading for more painkillers." I felt quelled and, as if on cue, the pain resumed with intermediate force and I was snatched back upstairs to begin my career. In no time they had fixed the usual ritual apparatus to my belly and seemed to be waiting for something. Now it appeared it was Dr. Vohra again with grim fatidic expression. He hurried to my bedside and began asking questions quite without his usual plenitude. He stopped suddenly and asked, "Am I addressing the cricketer and literary master Paul West?" I said, "I met you several times before." He said, moving right on as if I'd know him for years, "I was reading your Oxford book just now."

Well met indeed.

He resumed auscultating my body with a fraction more care, or did I imagine it? Surely he'd had enough to pick on, from blood in the urine and all else. And from that moment, or thereabouts, I had difficulty in determining faces and plainly was not to be trusted with anything medical. I was in some kind of internment camp where in spite of the comforting beds and the warm climate, I was now an unlicensed being.

V

I wonder if Sanjeev Vohra sensed that our paths
would cross again. An elementary operation to be
sure, but one to which he brought, as I was rapidly
learning, a finer element of trust than some of his
colleagues. I marvel at this transport of the here and
now because for most of it I was in a dream state, little
knowing whether I was discharged the next day or
brought to book for a serious offense against life itself.
Somewhere during these transitions Sanjeev changed
stations from being a duty-bound cricketer and fan of
the arts to being an apostle of rectitude. Lamentably,
I know little of this change of attitude, because, as I
said, my view of the world and its picture was being
subdued by the exotic latitudes of space. I know and
I do not know, but one thing is for sure: he moved
into my life with at first a sideways motion that in the
fullness of time became something else.

"Stent," he said to one of the aides attending
my obsequies, and the operation began. Not much
of an operation really, except that he was feeding
the stent through the penis up the ureter and into
the kidney to open the flow of urine and pus that
a kidney stone was blocking. Once again Versed
was my friend, so I did not have any memory of this
procedure and I was not helped when I came around
to discover my old friend Foley nesting once again
in my intimate parts. And I had to make do with his
abstract presence because Sanjeev had already gone
away to tend to further acts of mercy and heroism.

I wheeled back to Room 423 in semi-jubilation
feeling that I had once again conquered the alien
odds and was free to go back to my masterwork on
Osiris, which was clucking away merrily during my
absence. I do not know how I was becoming rapidly
accustomed to the ways of the Foley catheter, and
this time I did not so much mind that the operation
(so-called, because he did not cut me) had been a
success.

No such luck. One seemed barely an
afternoon's grace. Sanjeev was on my tail again
because urine had been seeping into my body
cavity and would have to be stopped. That meant
removing the kidney stone. I was once again in
the semi-blissful state, on the one hand watching
my friend Steve Poleskie, who had rapidly formed
the habit of visiting each day, rhapsodize about his
forthcoming book about America's first balloonist
and, on the other, beginning to dread of an operation
that would for the first time go wrong. I attributed
my growing nervousness to the fact that this time
around there seemed to be more people, even in
the preliminary stages, from Brandt the cardiologist
and other specialists. The sensation that I was bound
for the big jump grew on me and for the first time I
was oblivious of Osiris. I felt certain that somewhere
in the bounds of an operating room there was a
big potion, black liquid, awaiting me, from which
I would take days to recover. As best I knew, the
operation went well. I have no memory of it, nor
would I in my heart of hearts wish one. I was back

in my old shooting gallery on Floor 4, not feeling
too bad, but authentically noticing that the Foley
had returned; my penis hurt, and my ureter was
sore to a quite tolerable degree. Happily I was on
oxygen again, a large combination of painkillers and
antibiotics. This was no place to receive the further
rejoicings of Steve Poleskie and celebrate his book
to be, but I did my best. Steve was on a wave and
nothing could hold him back from its enjoyment.
I felt like I'd been vouchsafed one of the forbidden
tricks of the universe, unique as fairy incunabula
and not one to be repeated often in my lifetime;
but the author of all this was once again Sanjeev,
who was rapidly ascending in my estimation to
something between a golden eagle and an intense
maestro. What had he done? He'd used a laser to
jab at the uric acid kidney stone until it exploded,
although leaving some detritus around and about
in my kidney, which could safely be left, so the
optimists among us theorized to themselves, or could
actually make their own way out of the body cavity.
He had supervised an explosion! My feeling about
this prodigious feat had some element of worry:
had he gone beyond himself and supervised the first
explosion known to man of an atomic body? But
no, this operation had been done hundreds of times
before, was not the slightest bit unique apart from his
cunning.

     Casting around in my admittedly fallible
mind for an epithet to cover his mastery of his art, I
dreamed he was the master of an eyelash whom no

blight might afflict. I had a similar sense of his being a master cricketer whose score was never inadequate and on whose vellum I set my stall.

VI

The healer of all my ills was of course Dr. Ann
Costello, who had presided over a variety of ailments
from pneumonia, diabetes, bronchitis, and sore
feet to heart trouble and such like things. She was
not only an internist proper, but she seemed to
have read everything and quite dignifiedly had her
fingers in lots of pies. She never slept, or such was
the assumption, for she had interests of the widest
range, from word puzzles to sending her children
to Latvia and other such unaccustomed places. All
this contributed to the aesthetic of a life lived in total
harmony and vigilant regard. She had a knack for
quietly attuning herself to whatever clinical situation
offered itself and somehow divining what was
wrong. I had seen this tendency in other doctors, but
only in restricted form. I do not know exactly how
she succeeded in producing a full-ballasted attack on
the subject with so little warning.

But so it was, and here she was as ever for
my latest foray into the realm. Of course, Sanjeev
was there as well, making in his more explosive way,
the same kind of quiet. But rest assured, they covered
the waterfront of spectral possibility, divining almost
the moment, par for the course, that my infection
would develop. For when Sanjeev made enthusiastic
noise, Ann made a calm one and vice versa. Indeed,
they seemed to have between them the whole
templum of medical art, all to my benefit I suppose.

Then I was shuttling back and forth between

daydream and no dream at all, and you would
have sold me on either side of the outcome. I was
not to know it, but three or four days I would pass
in this not unpleasant place of dreams. Whether
either doctor was present at my demise or survival,
I couldn't be exactly sure, but I was confident that
either had an almost magisterial presence that would
see me through. Where the recklessness of such
thinking comes from I do not know, but it comes
and leaves behind it a tortuous bouquet. Perhaps
in all medicinal rampages, we need such provident
overseers. Those that get them receive them, I
suppose; those who don't, don't.

At any rate, at the hands of Costello and
Vohra, I supplied my own needs, or that is how it
felt. So I descended and ascended from periods
of doom and gloom to spells of sunlight, first day
second day third day, with, as I surmised, the
whole team anxiously watching, including Diane
Ackerman, Stephen Poleskie, Jeanne Mackin, Chris
Furst and, to be sure, itinerant members of the
funeral cortège who roamed about Floor 4. In the
senses, then, I was dreaming, but I had plenty of
backup. What might be done with ethical largesse
might be done with hope.

I interrupt this catalog to mention another
matter equal in seriousness that exercised all of the
medical team. This concerned the serious business
of aspiration. If I were to take a drink from the wrong
kind of liquid, I would in all probability aspirate
and, having filled my lungs with fluid, choke and

die. This unseemly possibility has three stages. The first is pudding, which in no sense imperils you; the next is honey, which puts you in less jeopardy; third is nectar, and finally water, when you are dicing with life and death. If this all sounds like mumbo jumbo to an educated audience, it should not. For anyone intending to drink beyond his means, the risk of suffocation is high. For my own part, being on pudding as I was, I was consigned to eat chocolate pudding but shrank from eating the obscene mixture called pudding water, by which a mixture was made of water and thickener until the spoon was standing straight up. Such licentious behavior on the part of English pudding makers may surprise no one, but it may reveal to countless consumers of coffee, tea, and other drinks the perilous condition that they are subjecting themselves to if they drink water that goes down the wrong pipe.

To partner such lethal jinx with so apparently a silly outcome seems unworthy of high medical seriousness, but it is true that I was facing a double-barreled outcome, both serious. The juxtaposition of these two was less potentially fatal because, as I was reminded by all and sundry, I was awake during salient points of the procedure.

I hate to embarrass my helpers, but I remember nothing of this at all, not even the atomizing of the kidney stone out of my system, not even the farce with the water. I presume a good case would be made for being attentive to one another's systems, and it is only courteous to do so; but I cannot recollect either of these events or the trimming that goes around them, not even the brocade on Diane's dress or the trimming on Ann Costello's mustard dress. I sometimes wish we could go back to experience the moments, in and out of time, just for the joy or hell of it, maybe to provide a wider experience of the world. Alas, it was not given to me. That spell of three or four days, with only fragmentary peepholes into the heart of the experience, must suffice. It certainly was the longest period in my life in which I was nearly oblivious to everything, and it haunts me afterward to realize that just as everybody's attention was glued on me, for what must have been an unpardonable delay, my attention was elsewhere, and I was no more responsible for what I was doing or saying than Caliban's filibuster.

VII

Different from before, deeper, new embedded,
like emerging from statuary. It was more like, I
persuaded myself, emerging from hopeful dances
staged by Hopis in the wilds of Arizona or it was
as much like anything as a Mardi Gras conducted
in New Orleans. There is certainly something
festive about it, or it was like a combination with
all my friends dancing in celebration to see that I
had survived or, at least, had come back to them
in semi-recognizable form. Whatever way, it had a
mad sound to it, like some incorrectly controlled
vibraphone, and it seemed to be getting louder in
conjunction with the voices of all my friends as they
saw my eyes open and my teeth blink.

All was going to be well from now on. I
supposed it was just a matter of getting used to the
rhythms. I felt well enough to rise from my bed of
supposed pain and give them a demonstration of
how limber I could be. Not so: I fell back into the
waiting arms of the night nurse and from then on left
all arrangements of my body to him.

Now back in my well-groomed chamber
(maids had been at it in my absence), I once again
needed the charming whisper of the air conditioner
and the bottle of milk furtively supplied by my
favorite nurse, Rosa. This could go on for days, I
supposed, while my blood pressure returned to
normal and my appetite improved beyond the point
of starvation, which it had not done so far. I'd gotten

into the habit of rejecting most forms of food on account of my fear of choking. The daily bottle of milk was my only friend, and that was by the good graces of the Borden Dairy.

This jolly-seeming interval took me through a couple of days, by which time I was chafing to be home, and I made no secret of my needs. Besides, it was glorious blue sky outside, and now I regarded myself as one of the healthy. But no again. Both Dr. Ann and Dr. Vohra wanted another period, which worked its way into yet another period. And so on down the line until I thought I would be there forever. Again I got to work on my manuscript about Osiris, and even started tasting portions of ham sandwich. Some friends had asked the same question testing my faith in Doctors Costello and Vohra: had they discovered some new tungsten factor in the matrix or some new radioactive substance in the stents?

VIII

One other way of comforting my bedraggled self
was to imagine it in the widest possible context.
Not just revealing it to the outer atoms, but to the
grand galaxies and even those spaces beyond the
likes of which, so often assumed, but so rarely seen,
in their exact detail. Of course, such a theatre was
optical, and could be relegated to a piece of the
slipstream. It was all a matter of comparative illusion,
best taken care of by some poor sucker anxious for
cosmic aggrandizement, especially when their own
version of justice had fallen into disrepute. Of course
such operations, although made much of, tended
to be purely mental and did not withstand exact
placement in the world of physics.

But every now and then a desperate man
comes along and calls the world to order exactly
as it requires. The same could be attributed to his
legs, kidneys, and intestines or what have you;
the urgency of arrangement could be decreed by
his need. It is not the first time in history that an
astronomer had felt the need to place a planet that
was not there.

Similarly, an enterprising artificer could
conjoin bits of himself all over the world to address
his dissatisfaction with the home front. I had not
realized, until now, the pleasure of this roaming
around history to place a planet or a galaxy whenever
one wanted, but it was a fetching idea; one that
delivered full force every time I looked at me.

Would it regain its normal shape or come back to a semblance of that? Looking at it in the light almost persuaded me that it was degenerating piece by piece, atom by atom, even as I looked at it, and was about to set me down in a place far inferior to the place I had already inhabited. But there was no predicting, and once again I felt the old absence of life, by which I mean its inclination to go wherever it wanted with humans tagging along for the ride.

It was next to impossible to read that far out into the Milky Way, just as it was next to impossible to read that far into a piece of me subjected to all the antics of the same body. Perhaps a lively consort of ideas would be illustrated by such placements of celestial bodies, but only so long as they remained utterly free to do their best or worst with us. Such obtuse speculations appealed particularly to my present mood since I seemed to be dealing with something that, although not pleasant and with a horrendous future in sight, threatened always to go somewhere, and not know where.

Thus equipped with a bountiful zeal, I sought to go on. Now as a piece of the mainstream and not of the slipstream, I wished with all my heart that a modicum of the world about us might be based on my own convenience for a change.

Perhaps I was exaggerating, but I sensed the feeling of one for the other. It was a fleeting feeling, no doubt, but one that reassured me. If I could dream my way into the secret arcana of stents, I could also dream my way into human meat. Indeed, meat, raw or cooked, was fast approaching the status of a delicacy in my mind, because I had at least meat to dream about, and what is a meat dream to a dream of bone, when you have no one to back it up?

Thus now equipped with a rude and hand-made philosophy, I faced the rising sun with new humility based on a new appreciation of my status. I wanted to be out of my present fix, you can be sure of that, but I also wanted, if I was stuck with it, to be as sentient an observer as possible, and to allow as much of an accommodation as possible. I realize this isn't much to hope for, but it is a lot more than nothing, and maybe a lively dance step could be executed upon it with some attention to detail and a reverence for the tango.

I have always wondered at the disproportion in our lives. For instance, the slight degree to which we go downhill everyday, prompted by this or that, compared with the massive onslaught of our bodies as a whole. I do forget in the midst of all this, the possibly benign effects when things look up, or look on the grand scale lively; it's a matter of what you are used to, and the direction always seems to be downward unless you are very keenly attuned to the mechanics of slight beings or huge crescendos. I imagine most people will think the other way, copping the little and big as a matter of course. Such people will often find that talking in such terms amounts to fool's gold of the worst order, abandoning them to a couple of false premises when they should have the bounty of creation.

I take refuge in a question voiced to me early on in my recovery phase: "Can you think without words?" The question surprised me; could I think in such abstruse terminology? What did amount to thinking, in these terms, moored between a rock and a hard place? I tried to imagine myself trapped with an inaudible voice coming out of nowhere and going nowhere with no result on faces of the listeners. What would choplogic invent next?

I tried to listen again to the phantom innuendo of speech without sound, and did detect a *soupçon* of Irish lilt coming to me from a thousand years away. This was surprising, to say the least, and I first wrote it off as an audible challenge not to be taken seriously. Then I tried again, wondering what it was that I was listening to. Was it what the poet Keats called the "spirits ditties of no tone?" (Ample proof that he had some investment in this line of country.) I could not, however, base my newfound art form on Keats alone. Still it was there: tenuous, rather shrill, and as far as I could detect . . . pure gibberish. Was I then to leap out, as far at least as my leash permitted, and announce to the world I had found a new mode of speech—inaudible, and incomprehensible? According to me, if any surreptitious art form of this kind existed, it should at least present itself and its argument in orthodox prose.

To be sure, what I was hearing was a big advance on what I was used to hearing. Gibberish instead of nothing (and Irish gibberish at that). My dilemma came to this: could I adapt my latest

discovery to the uses of language or was I doomed
to take on another supplementary art form just as
meaningless as my other one? Could my search for
a supplementary private language bear fruit? Could
I by complete inactivity force the language to give
up its true colors and come into view as specimen of
what John Keats was thinking of? I had gotten myself
into a philosophical fix such as my Roman ancestors
had merely dreamed of.

Once having heard this sublime, creaky,
and voxless voice, could I be doomed to hear it
ever afterward? Was there no way to shut it down?
I once again tried to listen in a more refined way
to its verbal footsteps, and I heard the authoritative
tones of an altogether different idiom, more like
language after all. I could not transliterate what the
voice was saying, but in the depths of my newfound
delirium I knew what it was saying. I was being
offered three things: pure silence, pure gibberish,
and an obscurative form of English, now and then
broken into by a form of Irish lyricism. Clearly I was
to choose, but not all three.

I could hardly believe that two exercises in
nonsense had partnered up with a third exercise
of occasional English. What was this occasional
helpful voice that came and went like an owl's
screech, although much toned down, and plagued
my ears with intimations of a language I seemed
to have lost? Perhaps the spirits were sending me a
consolation prize to mock the absence of what I had
lost. Or perhaps I was getting messages from the fifth

dimension from people whose previous messages had been unable to get through or had otherwise been lost. Or had my intermittent excursions into oral history been the messages sent at wartime that had not been sent through? There were other such theories that I could not trouble myself with.

What *was* the gist of my otherwise thrice-repeated messages from outer space? It was almost like asking what *is* outer space? The question had very little meaning. What was I then to do with such a soft-shuffle encouragement? This message with an Irish lilt disowned me after an hour and never bothered me again. Only to be replaced in coming days with yet another mode of speech, probably attuned to what I considered in my antique way, the voice of such an announcer as John Snagge of the BBC, a voice clear, manicured, and slightly arch.

Now where did *that* come from, assailing me in its friendly Irish? Was this the guest of a mere hour and would it be replaced by a third, fourth, and fifth entity, like a Berlitz course in world languages, all to no purpose? I still could not speak a single word, although my dreams were being rapidly infiltrated by ghost voices over which I had no control. The original asker of the question, long forgotten by now, had to go away unsatisfied because he had heard nothing at all of this series of quiet transits among the neighboring stars.

I hasten to remind readers that in all my wanderings I had never refused to take a reference or an index as far as it would let me, theorizing as I do

that he who takes a bee's width, when he is offered
a star like Ultima Centauri to feast from, is doing
his side a bad turn. The voices did persist, although
often diminished in frequency, and I came to call on
them whenever I wanted a change of vision. The next
putative voice I heard would in all probability be the
voice of my first word, recognizable or not. Such at
any rate was my theory, and I believe that I was so
optimistic as to think it would more likely be a word
than gibberish.

IX

At another level, however, things bright and metallic
would not go away. An old order had asserted
itself. Let no one doubt my zeal to be agitated: the
vibrations of the fibers, the agitation of the pulses,
the weird pulsing of the noises in my ears, ringing
noises in my head as the world tried to come to
rights between earth and heaven.

I, who had been a little slothful, had become
more than a little agitated. It was really a matter of
what came next. In the old days it seemed a toss-up
between what came next, and did not matter that
much, and a bright insistent message that everything
was all right. Now it was a matter of never knowing
what came next, and the bright bandana of
possibility somehow became stunted as a result.

The heavens still had their music, though
a scratchier kind, to which I still listened intently
when I could. Added to this, however, was sleek
indeterminacy, which sent the heavenly bodies
off center and made my pilotage pretty much a
torment. To this I added a twitchiness of the eyes, as
if continually going to see something that I would
prefer to bypass. Besides, I had a twitchiness of the
limbs that must have counted for something but only
recently seemed to be a mild form of Saint Vitus's
dance.

There were other phenomena, too, from a
shaking sound in my head to a noise like tea leaves
from somewhere in my lumbar region. Not quite

distressing, although these sounds could not help but suggest the multiplicity of sounds there *could* have been. I add to this belfry of quiet sounds the tinkling that roamed around my head, driving me to think I had become one of the elect. Or the belfry sounds would decrease and drive me mad with delight.

Such sounds and noises belonged presumably to no one else, and in that I could take pride. But it all sounded like too much of a good thing, and I more than once yearned for a quiet world, akin to the world that once blighted me. All the same, I clung to fragments of this world, not least to the taste of something in my mouth, a taste balsamic and crude, which I homed onto with all the rapture of a man touching for the first time his toothache in the night.

I add to this a strange sensation in my good arm. The fingers were not as sensitive as they should have been. Similarly, my fingers felt partially deprived of their quick response to anyone trailing a hair across them or bouncing a balloon on them to test for diabetes. It was not the old sensation as before, which could easily have been pleasant, so stylish was the touch of those fairy fingers. It was simply a brutalization of those tiny tempi to something not as joyful as before but duller and more opaque.

If you add the topic of touch to this merry-go-round of the black night, you may find a phenomenon almost impossible to describe, a feeling that my whole body, though not being case-hardened, had become more defiant to touch. It was not an unpleasant sensation but as if I had converted to something stiffer. I am aware of sneaking in many surreptitious references to the piano, glancing references to my mother the pianist, and here is another one: something starker and more mahogany-hued has been added to the mix. And whether it makes it easier to play, whether the keys go down with a firmer punch or lift upward with a genuinely soft touch, I have no idea.

Besides, such divisions approximate only a tenth of an inch, if that. In any case, that is not my initial concern because I am not playing the piano anyway. And in fact never played it after my first stumbling performances, much to the initial distress of my mother, who wished she had a pianist and not a novelist in the family.

A sentient observer would find, perhaps will find, that here is a case of a man who has come around from repeated delirium to observe the minute changes in his world. True. I've been overloaded with minute changes, some ever to be ignored as the big bustle of everyday living takes charge. I sense in the complex fabric of my being that I have been remarkably changed, which is not to say that the changes have been wholesale and discounted, but that they have been irrevocable and final.

X

I've been reconsidering my statements about my
convivial overtures to fortune. I may have given
the impression that these were a crescendo of
panegyrics. Not so. Like the French existentialists,
now of a different generation, you may be forgiven
for thinking that all was action to them and that
thought had little place in their activities. You
imagined them, if you imagined them at all, racing
from one hare-brained scheme to the next, with
little concern for either propriety or warning. Such a
hectic lifestyle may be all right for 1940s Frenchmen,
but not for deciding how to load the next bale.

In a word, the dominant emotion was panic,
not for you the blithe conversion to this or that lively
self-assertion but a shift from panic to a timidity
and back again, finally emerging in several hours to
sheer timidity and able to go on for hours more. So
that any given sleepless night, you were capable of
only four or five general statements embodying your
philosophy. The rest is filled with rustic incertitude,
which is when the inclination of an idea meets the
disinclination, and so it goes nowhere at all for
hours. And sometimes days. This current of nerves
faltering and of indecisive meandering will produce
nothing very slowly, although the resulting mental
turmoil may be fast and loose up to a certain point;
then all will collapse like a house of cards until the
next sequence of lost hope.

If you prefer to think of it in larger terms,

then you could say a part of each typical week would yield some twenty discoveries. This means, with due allowance paid for duplication, one or two bright hours per week. So anyone tempted to imagine several radiant hours of nonstop thought, even for those of us who bear the consequences of this or that stroke, may be in for a heart-wrenching disappointment. It is hard to persuade anyone that the life of man can be so bald and unproductive for weeks on end, but the truth is that a large number of us spend much of our time getting nowhere at all and fattening up our internal systems with fat nothings. I suppose this is a brutal fact for the avid student learning the books by night and day, but these once insistent lives are easily swept under the rug and have no place in lively discourse.

So one who entertains the vision of all points mustering to one final electric point can be disappointed again and again, for it does not happen. And many of these people go on to think less and less until one day they conclude operations in the final wave of blank inattention. It's terribly hard to psych out these people whose mental impotence leads continually to naught, but they rank among the heroes with the paradox of the fortunate Fall behind them. Or to put it another way, they rise to a point unbelievably high and distinguished for all their toil but fall back the last minute as the earth begins to crumble around them, equipping them with less than they had before. This process repeats indefinitely, I suppose, until nature itself takes a hand

and reduces the sufferer to a species of morbidness. Abandon hope, all ye who enter here.

You can see that such a career may well lead to panic or to huge contraction. A small idea disguised as a word is not a word at all. For instance, *Robitracing* or my own word *Turps*. It is not a matter of seemly adjustments but much more one of panicky adaptation to something that for the time being anyway is completely false. I think that, having registered this point, what matters is the insufficiency of the falsity in what is offered to the sufferer. If he spends the rest of his days eyeing the same nonword then let him. He has already, in part or in whole, charged the burden with life.

The question becomes not what he has any longer but what he has not—ridiculous to contemplate when you reckon up all the fine formulations and provident speculations of his previous career. When all is said and done, this is still his battered career. He has been used by life and found in the category that now makes no sense; and his joys, if anything, are little mundane things, reaching from what he panics to remember because he has again forgotten it to the joys of the World encompassed in a single word.

I realize that in painting this I am doing a disservice to all those people who can still think for themselves. Good luck to them. I think it worth reminding people of the degree to which we all fall down. Having been for a month part of the nervous, faltering, nervously interior-brooding people in one hospital, I recur time and again to what I've seen in there and to what spartan regimes people have subjected themselves to.

I do not like to contemplate what nullity does to people. The long struggle back for the lucky ones, learning to walk with spavined and unserviceable brains. But I accept these hammer blows of creation as overdue and in the long run accept them as part of the mystery that Galileo spoke of when arguing that people simply had to be dispatched for other people to displace them.

One wishes always for the happy growing of the planets together, within prescribed limits and proscribed extents. What happens in fact, try as we may, is a mixture of the two, sandwiching failure and success in roughly equal portions, usually failing as one gets older. As an old friend of mine used to say, "Life ends at forty and suffering begins." Or it ends much sooner than that. The problem, as I've found, is to give the little vital commoners, as Shakespeare puts it, their due, half suspecting their little chirpings and cheepings would eventually lead to disaster and therefore half supplying their success.

I first turned my attention to the head, as one should when anything meaty is at hand. Was it growing at all? In which direction, if so, and what little could I do to control it? I fancied that it was growing outward just a speck, basing my opinion on nothing more important than little shreds of meat. There was certainly a twinge, now and then, which I immediately gave over to the prosperous side of the business. I said *speck*, when a better term would have been *atom* or *molecule*, but I am not ready for niceties at this point. The least little hint I received that the balance was going in my favor cheered me no end and would not be gainsaid.

Who is to tell of the adventures of a fraction of meat in the exploit of a carnivore? Put simply, my nervous system put me in the minute minor repetition of things that had happened throughout history and would go on happening. It was like being tugged by an ant in the presence of an elephant and gave to my only-too-willing positive inclination a hearty tug toward sanity.

I began to dote on this tugging, which averaged three or four impulsions a day, as my ticket to the future, little as could be said for it in the larger scope of things. I attended, and the tugging began all over again, but only to the tune of a handful each day. I suppose I am guilty, in some lethal final court, of wishful thinking; by this idealizing of my destiny I was playing into the hands of a more insidious fate than I could ever have imagined.

Let us just say I soldiered on from one day to another as best I could, still mute, hoping for some chance of saying something simple again. This is, of course, a mark of sanity, proving yourself when all is up for grabs and thus fooling yourself much of the time about a little lame patch of meat. I nonetheless proposed to myself that the rate of advance was quickening, say three atoms instead of two the first day, and maybe four the next.

Whether one can sustain over a period of months such a hoax, I do not know, or whether hoping will make it so. I jollied on toward my eternal reward, which looked a thousand years into the future and was predicated on the belief that God was on the side of the strongest artillery.

There was another misgiving to my enterprise. Suppose the repetitive impulses and the inner workings of my physique themselves turned inward, not working on my behalf but promoting the destruction and turmoil of it all? Suppose they launched an all-out attack on my metabolism, a poor word for something as beleaguered and duck-shot as could be found. I even had small-scale rehearsals of such an event. Resting while still immobile, my heart refused to go where my mind did not and harassed me from afar with all the weapons in its possession. This said, you have no chance of winning against such an awesome galaxy of stars. Best submit while you have a chance. I heard them, but only in the distant fumble of the sea, gleaning what little I had to hold on to.

Only a fool can gather the volley of forces against him in this way. Only a blind fool can assemble the light forces that support him against despair. I did, though, sleepwalking my way through it blindfolded; and I trusted not so much to luck as to something else that I could not find the words for but that, in the ultimate hegemony of all things promised, would appear. If this seems a paltry thing to rest my faith upon, so be it. It was all I was provided with, and heavily tilted to one side, as I later realized.

When I at last began to believe time was exerting a diminished pressure on my face, I believed other things would follow if I lived long enough to see them prosper. For there was doubt. There was always doubt. You could no more depend on such a promise than you could depend on Harpo Marx's discovering another brother. I would not say I regained my sense of humor at that point, for I had never lost it except when unconscious, but I rescued from the jaws of oblivion the tiny shreds of a promise. What is a shred to a thunderbolt, if the shred persists and the thunderbolt continues its mournful patrol to the edge of the known world and perishes with a whimper and satiated glory?

XI

Drawn as I am to the fascinations of the tardigrades,
I am never enticed by their mere slowness. Which is
to say, I don't like things rushed, prefer some things
rendered immobile to the point of not moving at all,
as with the petty movements on the human scale. So
long as the movement is away from me, I don't mind
how slow it is. Whether this boils down to a sea
change you cannot see is a matter of indifference to
me and is likely to remain so.

I realize that in committing myself this way
to a future of slowness, I am saying that I don't mind
how slowly atoms grow. If this suggests a perpetual
slowness in the affairs of life, then it must be all I
care about, fixed as I am, the slowness of things
racked against their inevitability. I have had enough
things either stationary or rushing pell-mell to care
much more about their final ranking. If I can have, in
perpetuity, a slug instead, that will do for me, even if
it takes the rest of civilization to get where it's going.

I suppose I'm with the tardigrades for this
admission, and it seems the slow-whiskered, bare-
boned, and paltry-sinewed ones as well. I suppose
you can want some things in slow motion and all the
rest top speed, but I doubt it and find if the one goes
slowly then all the rest do as well.

As I say in my newfound jubilation, so long
as motion is on my side, all is well. I admit to taking
not much account of skin, whiskers, bones, sinews,
and all the rest as a result. This is careless of me, no

doubt, but one cannot always be susceptible to the
finer points of human anatomy. A shrewder judge
than I will find all the members of his echelon going
at the same pace, and good luck to him.

This is about the extended use of a body part
that has lain useless or distorted for too long, and
once the blissful movement has started up, there is
no gainsaying it. So here I am, with the fine sensation
of my bum growing outward but one millimeter
per week and concentrating on not much else. I
suppose this makes of me an insipid monomaniac,
but so what; I have earned my right to lounge about
in this way, even if the rest of the quest takes me to
Zanzibar and back. There are some privileges that
are out of this world, and I relish not going back to
them.

Of a different kind entirely are those simple
exercises known to us as body contact sports, from
broken bones to punctured eardrums. These are the
hopeful gestures of people who expect to be righted
and sent back to action with renewed vigor. One has
met them everywhere. Contrast these sports with the
invincible meat masters plying their trade to the end
of time, neither hoping for too little nor hoping too
much. They seem like companions or conjoiners,
but they are not. One rides the infliction of the
temporary injury, while the other rides the permanent
disgrace of the wound that will not be finished with
him before his number is called.

XII

Various others have told me how I raced through
several doorways in pursuit of an exit. Either I sidled
through or worked the door in a long blast of would-
be freedom. For remember, I was still the owner of a
good pair of legs, thinned out as you would expect.
Sometimes I caught the two auburn-haired sisters
who officiated as guardians off guard and managed
to go all the way into the major hallway. Sometimes,
thanks to these same sisters, I was trapped before
I had begun. Sometimes, on at least one or two
occasions, I penetrated the major hallways and
then spent the few minutes of my precious freedom
looking in vain for a door that would lead down into
the outside world. The sisters quickly got used to my
midnight forays and became adept at cutting me off
before I reached the outer anteroom, either trapping
me with a paillasse or running me to ground in one
of the lavatories. It was a jaunt for the full body. In
one way I looked forward to being captured and
restored to my bed and told for the umpteenth time
to stay there or they would not be responsible for my
safety.

One day I continued on my vagrant ways
and suddenly found that somebody had removed
all my clothes. I was a naked runner and maybe
gained an extra inch or two of speed from that, as I
saw it. I was fit enough to run, although naked, and
in good enough condition to escape with a military
salute, the next destination all the way home, where

my books and other treasures awaited me. Clearly some renegade part of me was still tinged with lunacy: I saw the problem as only extending between the way out and the way home. There were many hurdles in between that I would have to jump, one by one. The mad dasher over the parquet floor was to become the sagacious intellect of Floor B7. I am sure now that the impulse to dash madly about was inspired by the lull between 5 a.m. and breakfast time when there was nothing to do and all kinds of forces were arrayed against you. Had that not been the explanation, I would not have risked all those incomplete early morning adventures, either sliding to a gliding halt or cannoning to a stop above either sister's iron-hard bosom. They never caught me anyway. I did not find the entrance to the way out, and always they returned me, with wagging fingers and nagging expressions, to my bed.

It was vain to point out to me the dangers of it all. I had certainly not been cut during any of this, but there were all kinds of things going on in my system, and these the staff pointed out to me. I was mute still and had no business scooting around the halls, either naked or clad. And I was further reminded of the eleven or thirteen chemicals that wandered about in my breast, some of them impervious to what I put them through in my nightly excursions, some definitely not. I decided to be a good boy and work my passage outward as good boys do.

For contemplation's sake, I took to reviewing

my body at its most wholesome. Legs, arms, and maybe even some portions of my afflicted eyes would serve as a beginning. I considered it not bad to have survived with these and, for a change, decided to write in big letters the bits of my body that had survived. A pleasurable excursion, no doubt, to which I could return. It was a matter of looking always on the bright side, until you were looking no longer; in this way, unless you were singularly unfortunate, you always had something to admire. But, of course, the satanic and brooding always ousted the healthy and suspicious, perhaps because we merely tired as a nation of the life-affirming. Which strikes me as utterly extraordinary, considering all that people have wrong with them. I have always been fascinated with the dark side of humanity, maybe because so many maligned works of infamous subjectivity therein repose.

XIII

So at last we find that something has given way in
the decorous image we call a mouth. Hunting time
is here again and, for a moment, extravagant images
of men in red jackets stream across an invisible
landscape until they fall from my eyes into the
Slough of Despond. In spite of the hunting image,
and all it carries with it of red cheer and hunting
bells, I need to attend and examine what progress
has been made. I just have this feeling of something
that was not there yesterday, unidentifiable, but
something different maybe by one iota or one
millimeter, something with a specific meaning for me
and due to be ferreted out.

Before beginning, however, I try to imagine
something incredibly preposterous, such as the one
millimeter high-wire act sustained by a rabbit or,
harking back to my previous image of huntsmen,
a body of men in red jackets who at some point
merge and become one, dwindling to the size
of a red iota, then vanish. I restore my senses to
gravity by surveying the landscape of my head and
wondering which of its unruly scenes has sponsored
this change. I glance downward at the space where
one cheek looms larger than the other, casting my
eye, as much as I can, for any vital change of scene.
But nothing comes to mind, mainly owing to lack
of visibility. You cannot do this if all you have is a
pair of conventional cheeks. You can do this only if
one of the cheeks is distended, and not much is to

be gained by that. All the same, I screw up one eye, then peer down in a fresh orientation that actually seems to profit the view. I still cannot see anything unusual, though, and I was getting my hopes up to the point of a jubilant fulsomeness that evaporated almost as soon as it began. Somewhere in my skin, I was convinced, whenever I tried to formulate a sentence or word, maybe it would take a year to find it, by which time the situation would have righted itself in any case. But the mottled skin that met my eye revealed nothing apart from a touch of dryness. At this point I seemed to lose heart and, after a last look at the sallow underpinning of my mood, relinquished the cheek for the open-air delights of a pound and a half of raw flesh, which promised better hunting.

This game resembled the cheek sighting in no fashion at all. First, I was of course imagining flesh whereas I could see the cheek. Somewhere in that vast pericardium of mine, I would be certain to find the starting point I was looking for. It may take a year, I said to myself, in echo of what I said about the cheek, but it would be worth it to have on the premises this fiendish extrapolation of one blood cell. I once abandoned the skin for the flesh and spent what seemed like an hour, or it could have been almost a day, looking at and poring over scenes of imagined flesh that would have done Mr. Lon Chaney proud.

All good dreams come to an end. I switched suddenly from blood to muscles, hoping that with my third excursion into the hinterlands of my rapidly wearying self, I would find a prospect of unmitigated joy. Unlikely as muscles seemed to promise any such thing, I kept faith with them until I had an alarming thought: I did not know what they really looked like, apart from a glimpse of some white matter oozing between what looked like diminutive caterpillars. I did not know where I was, and I thought that of all the hard things in the world that remained to do, iota or millimeter hunting was the worst, and the worst of all the rest of them was the maggotlike muscle. I abandoned it after unsuccessfully persuading it to yield up its secret.

I was left with bone, though God knows what other parts of my anatomy I had scanted in my survey. Bone suggested a painting by Henry Moore, but that was not the way to go. Imagine a man sinking to atom size or millimeter size, in an oasis of bone. Where other things had the prudence to clothe themselves up, bone preferred to divest itself of human apparatus and ride the back roads of history with a continuous shout of triumph.

I dimly perceived that all this shuffling about between my eyes was no good. Imagination had to bring the solution to me. The body parts I had in mind were exercising themselves in consort, not in concert, and the con*sorts* had it over the con*certs*. Perhaps from some old tradition of helping each other out, without combining.

Once again I saw the irresistible futility of thinking for myself. Who cared that on a whim I had been chasing an almost invisible piece of particulate matter around the houses and over the hills. I was discovering all over again the aloneness of man in his finest literary endeavors, and who would blame him for getting as much out of it as he could and then damning the whole experience as an expense of spirit and a waste of shame.

Lovely summer was beckoning me to join her at home in the pool beyond the pagoda. If this was an illusion, it was a precious one, and one that spoke to the core of my being much more than a flick of matter had ever done. I missed swimming even more than I missed music, and I wondered if I could not someday soon persuade somebody to wheel me down to ground level to feel the sun on my face as never before. How did one apply for this privilege? And if so, to whom? I reviewed my situation and, in the most benign manner possible, wondered why a man in my condition, seemingly getting better, had not been accorded this delight before now. I was far from feeling the athletic performer I should have been but, I was far from dead and could be relied on to at least navigate the patio chair into an open space where the sun beat down with its old authority upon my badly tousled head. Once in position, I could stay there forever, heedless of summonses to return to the Maginot Line of the main building to receive my twelve drugs.

Much was going on behind my back about my condition, but my feeling was that it was now more hopeful. I could not give chapter and verse on

these discussions, however, because I was not privy
to them but was included in some talks as a matter
of courtesy, except when the talk was grave. I heard
my assorted fate clearly expounded or strategically
whispered and garbled; in fact, it didn't make a lot of
sense.

It's true that some friends and doctors
busied themselves around me, almost successfully
persuading me to eat or to take my pills like a
gentleman. Diane, who had not only been visiting
me but sleeping alongside me in those terrible
nights, had now changed schedule to one of morning
visits and evening visits and, for the time being at
any rate, slept at home, where she got enough sleep.
So actually I had more free time on my hands, either
to entertain myself in the dark between the hours of
3 a.m. and 7 a.m., which was difficult, especially for
a visionary such as I who had horrible memories of
meeting himself going back and coming forward all
at the same speed, to no purpose.

The other period was easier to negotiate, for
I had more to do, which charitable observers might
describe as increasing demands upon my time. But
I never thought the merest smidgen about music in
all the time I was in rehab. Now it burst forth, from
my micromini set, like a noise I'd never heard before,
recognizable but impossibly weird, like something
Delius might have written in one of his most
romantic moments, crisscrossed with something by
Schoenberg. I listened, rapt, for some time until I was
awakened to go and play skittles, which, when I got

there, turned into a game of soccer without warning, with two of us instead of eight, the only two patients with competent legs. Such a clash with Delius-Schoenberg was unthinkable, and I heard the strains of both above the usual football noises.

I soon got back to the music and played the radio intermittently until Diane arrived with dinner, sacrificing me on the altar of another piece of blameless salmon. The only dishes I deigned to eat were a chocolate pudding and fried bread, with occasional pumpings of hot cocoa. And the debate about my increasing loss of weight was driving at least two of my doctors into the finer recesses of their discipline. I had been warned, however, about the dangers of swallowing food at all, little though I understood that, and the message had stuck. Into the bargain, I thought it might give the simian people who were attending my fate an extra incentive to send me home from the esoteric wasteland called rehab.

I returned to my study of Delius-Schoenberg, who had now become Roussel and Beethoven, a more illustrious pair by far. And allowed to mingle in my headset, in a most amazing way, the lilt of the music, the sound of swimming from far away and just within earshot, and the language of an at-last-appreciated meal of lion steak. I had still not been cleared to the Shangri-la of the swimming pool, but I was convinced that I would soon, after I had perhaps amazed them with a blaze of glorious eating. We would see. For the rest, I would resume

my interrogation of the dulcet harmonies of no tone
that haunted my body in such a dull way. You see, I
still had various brands of hope, coming from several
sources. The situation would get better, would it not?
And I would once again be launched on the world
as a fully speaking ogre and a man whose right arm
could be pirouetted to an amazing height above the
element it soared in.

XIV

So the days went by, always repetitive and short
of sleep. The skies were a bright blue and seemed
to promise a liquid form of themselves, a brighter
blue than ever. Was this the sky I dreamed about
in my crèche, now warning me of days to come in
my solid, leaden state as I brooded on the primrose
and other summer flowers? The world, in which I
half heard the cry of Inderal (a beta-blocker) as if it
were a crow, was promising to be a better place. A
securer, more reliable, and trustworthy place. My
senses kept me in an emotional, nearly ovational
state.

So there was some logic, as I fancied, in my
imagining the sky as a potent blue. It was seeping
out, this blue, to all prismdom; it had been arranged
for me on a personal basis as a choice exhibit of the
universe at its most rigid and controlled. There was
something imaginative in this twin, something that I
had not been aware of before, and something that I
welcomed as one of the first samples of grace.

I must expand these notes to show what a
strange thing relief was, coming out of the matrix of
horror and devastation, with me cruising along at no
speed per hour and in the process being hurled from
one nightmare to another. I will not pretend that
all was well during this indeterminate period, but I
can best illustrate it when I say that I heard a cry of
Inderal pretending to be the anti-hypertensive Cozaar
and of Cozaar pretending to be Inderal. (Or even of

Cozaar pretending to be Cortázar!) The prevalence of one drug over the other didn't matter. Perhaps they were interchangeable, perhaps they were not. But why, if they were interchangeable, were there two of them? The sense I had of either's being a leaden, sultry bivalve lingered on. I had discovered the interchangeability of matter, or close to it, and somehow it made things better than before. I report here only that the mere association of myself with these beings, whatever they were, had a brightening effect too long held in abeyance.

I associate this sense of quickening with the equal thought of being tired; I tired quickly, although in a kind of ecstasy, from which I rose tired again though just as ecstatic. Perhaps this was the dead end of the world that you survived eminently. Fortunately, it seemed wise to accept this Kabbalistic sign as one of those sedate warnings from history: not to expect too much but to be content with nothing going wrong.

I remain unsure whether this was an old muddle or a new muddle. I was content to leave it at that for the time being. It was clear to me, in its hazy way, that a message had been vouchsafed to me and what was positive in it would have to do. Indeed, there was the matter of fending such messages at speed: they were over so quickly that you might spend the rest of your days waiting for the next one or vexing the one you had, worrying lest you had misinterpreted. I confess to having misdiagnosed it in a state almost of uncustomary levity, arguing with myself that a maligned organism would not have sent in any bad news in the first place. Such, you see, was the extent of my knotty porings over my cosmic fate, reducible always to a quick swat but also convertible to a bright, almost blistering bugle of human matter.

XV

Something grounded. Something stabilized.
Something marked even for my own consumption.
That was how I faced up to my new fate, sensing
in the air about me a flavor like mint. I could not
be wrong this time—after all those other times of
relenting, shameful fastidiousness. It was no longer a
matter of something firmer and trustworthy beneath
my feet. It was not that simple at all. Indeed, the
emanation that came from my head had a lilt about
it that could not in any way be attributed to my head.

If life were going to be as simple as that,
things would be certain to improve. It might take
a year or more, but something bold in my head
would one day urge me to speak. It's easy to form an
obsession, making up in passionate addiction what
we lack in concentration.

This is to say, to hell with prosy statements
about numbness, or about anything else, for that
matter. It's all about what the self-sufficient man or
woman assembles to keep him- or herself awake,
and as far out as possible from the range of the
cur who roams the hinterland looking for food or
the equally mangy cur who confidently haunts the
bright, sunlit avenues of our city, scalpel in hand.
Sometimes the constant waiting and brisk incertitude
tires me out and provokes me. I grow hostile, to any
form of life. You let the shriek out and double up on
it until it is a goner and is quietly put to bed again,
beneath the latest down comforter.

I often wonder why the mind does not go blank more often. You would think that with so much to do it would welcome any respite that lies at hand. But no, my own experience shuttles back and forth between oblivion and talk, and the oblivion part is unfairly dropped. What gets you eventually is the waiting: after the initial period of waiting, there is more waiting and still more, until waiting suffers a sea change into something opaque and gruesome, not like the original forms of waiting at all, but delicate to touch. I think within my heartiest of hearts that something has changed; a little flick of time's chronometer or even an upward movement in time itself. Such things may easily defraud us into thinking something positive is afoot, whereas of course it could be the first stage in a downward cycle that promises the end.

I have no ulterior knowledge, though I have reasonably happy memories of Robert Browning's character "Pippa Passes" (this the title of the poem, she's Pippa), whom I remember, vaguely, was an expert on optimism. But you do not have to read Browning to glean something of his mood. You can get it from almost anywhere because people don't know, much of the time, what is happening to them anyway; they advance from darkness to darkness, from half suspension to something stronger, from ecstasy to nightmare, seen as a flash, until they emerge quite mesmerized by the changing scene and circumstances, to lose heart. Yet I know what I know, as the big, bloated commissioner once familiar from

German movies said, all bustle and bristle of the mustache. But now lost. Not much, almost enough to tide me over until the next.

XVI

One of the more entertaining diversions was to be
ferried along the interminable corridors of several
buildings to a pokey little room that was introduced
by its owner, Rebecca, as *my* room. Once we had
settled in, and once she had given me a half-cup
of what was rapidly becoming my favorite drink,
lemonade, we got to work. But not before she had
supervised my mouth in its troubled consumption of
the lemonade, which spilled half out. The object of
our attentions was the snappy little machine with lots
of counters and electric displays. I was marvelously
impressed at the outset with such an engine, for,
in my total ignorance, I thought the display was
something aeronautical.

I was rather disappointed to learn that it
was my old alien ally, the computer. And further
chastened when Rebecca, whose zeal was now
feeling the full thrust of power, explained to me
that this machine would help me to talk. I hasten
to inform the reader that I still had not said a
recognizable word. I burst out laughing at such a
suggestion. Surely she did not associate a man in my
condition with such an elaborate machine, although
in her bright, impetuous way, she looked capable of
handling any refractory machine, or even Roy's Vegas
night-club tiger, who had—or had not—mauled him.

"It's simple once you know how," said
Rebecca.

"MemmeMemmeMemme."

Visibly she was baffled by my wolverine reply. But like any well-trained speech therapist, she was consecrated to try, and try she did, coming up with a bewildering assortment of suggestions, none of which even approximated what I was trying to say, because I was too daunted by the presence of the computer and still prey to helpless laughter when I considered the enormous minified array of its keyboard.

She pointed to some arcane feature of the machine and said something about the ease with which I could teach the damn thing to write. But I could not see the numbers and letters. The orthography was not even in the accustomed order but was a ramble away from my trained eye.

What I'd tried to say, with only the usual hectic babbling, was, "I could not cope with this in a month of Sundays." But I stopped short. I had just discovered something leaning on my awareness for one or two days, which now was coming into what I presumed was the open. I was hearing, albeit silently, and with a sluggish droop, a high-toned music of the mouth, learned probably in some seminar of Matthew Arnold's years ago, which served me as a kind of language. I could hear a comradely chirrup.

She, having heard nothing, still looked like she expected me to utter some words, however disheveled they were, and put her out of her misery. Again, I tried in my voiceless way to communicate, but it was of no use. Instead I resorted to shaking my head violently at the machine and turning thumbs down at its procedures. She got the point and closed it up.

She was not a bad girl if you wanted speech therapy presented in a quite broad critical vocabulary and with a charm nobody denied. Her lucid elaborations of some point or other had been worked out time and again, and she was convincing. And was indeed being invited to decamp to a rival institution. She would not be here for long, I judged, and if I did not let her persuade me into trafficking with her typewriter machine, all was well.

The comical, grievous side to the conversation, now that we had dismissed the adding machine, was that we had nothing to talk about. I was dumb and she was prolix, which made for a bad and humiliating mix. She could lecture me on all kinds of speech subjects without my saying a word, and I had been, one way or another, doing too much of that of late. We might entertain bright repartees before she left for her new job, though she gave the impression of trusting me only so far, divining perhaps that I might at some point flash out with a corybantic dither.

Let us say that she reserved a silk eye-burst for me that would see me through even worse situations than I'd already encountered.

XVII

The chatter of A. J. Morpurgo's little feet sounded
again along the brittle hallway. This inspector of
men and women, usually so benign of aspect,
was supposed to take them far and wide in the
perambulations of his domain, leaving nobody
out. Properly executed, this maneuver would have
cost him four or five hours, so some visits had to
be shorter than others, customarily devoted in a
nondenominational way to the dying and the half
dead. The sight of his bow tie and unwrinkled shirt
always gladdened my heart because he seemed to
bring good tidings with him, and human society that
much nearer.

On this occasion he did not stay long, perhaps
because he faced once again the mute ghoul who
stared at him. With each visit he had some beneficial
novelty to impart. He must have tired of this one-way
conversation early on, for apart from wishing me the
"top of the morning," he withdrew and went pattering
down the hallway to his next visitation. I never grieved
for very long, because I would in all probability see
him on his afternoon rounds, when, just as dumb as
before, I would find him in a more gladsome mood.
To me, this round of his seemed perfunctory, although
it was executed at the same speed as his morning one,
maybe even a little faster. Either way, Morpurgo was
on his rounds again and could be relied upon, until
the end of time, to execute his sublime quickstep and
fox trot rhythm.

The machinery, as I call it, of the rehabilitation facility permitted among its gifts a three-foot cord that tied you to your bunk. The ward timed its victims asleep by 9 or 10 p.m., imposing on them a triple fiat that warned them the hour was now approaching. Had approached. And was gone. For most inhabitants of the ward, waking-up-time took place at three or four in the morning, which meant that, until breakfast was served at nine o'clock, the citizens had ample time to play with each other until they collapsed in a heap after breakfast when the day really began.

This was brutal discipline for the inmates, forcing them to disport themselves (such of them as could) to the rehab room, forcing them to indulge in calisthenics long before they could expect to sleep again. I fretted about this shift in time, equipping me with five or six hours free in which to plunge myself in the semidarkness or make an emergency toilet call, which would set the three wild women of cornucopia, wherever they came from, running after me in all directions to see that I assumed the right position for toilet training and subsequent absterging.

I never solved this problem of the schedule. What is more, they made it worse by ushering into my faintly lit bedchamber an armed man in a military uniform whose duty was to inscribe onto a black and white board, just out of reach, the program of the day. He wrote. I tried to watch but never got half the words. He went away. And I could not reach the blackboard without waking the whole establishment yet again. So I had to wait until a more appropriate hour for his *levee*. When I at last got to read the glad tidings of the day, I discovered that I had been scheduled from 8:15 a.m. (thus missing breakfast) for an interesting assortment of exercises ranging from bike riding, bobbing, and medicinal soccer to croquet and halma.

If these redoubtable exercises running from eight in the morning to five-thirty at night failed to bring the whipped corpse home on time, nothing would. The enterprising shirker could find ample space to play in (if he could only get past the guards on duty) and occupy himself with the limited grandeur of the rooms and hallways that stretched beyond anyone's imagination, all the way to the sunlit valley of the high tropics. It never happened. Some constraint held us back to the games room where we ended up lackadaisically tapping a ball about or, for those who could not walk, playing with blocks.

I often imagined, as a survivor, what life would be like without any of these nominal-seeming hindrances. There would be fewer staff and fewer nurses. There would also be a more rational attitude to the matter of the blackboard and the timing. How anybody could wake at three in the morning and be ready for a full six hours, including a hard bout of athletics lasting until dinner, eludes me entirely. But such places are not geared to be conveniences to man or any other species but are meant to make you obey, lest you spoil the machinery.

I often sent away urgent applicants pausing at my curtain with an imperious invitation to basketball, knee-jerk riding, or military calisthenics. They went, but with a sour grace, because according to their theory and practice, I was betraying the athleticist's vision of the supplicant or their vision of the program as a whole. On one occasion I had to wrestle a sports bimbo five or six times before she finally let go. And she still came after me, to exercise, on the day of departure.

Kind friends had offered me a range of swabs that were elementary lollipops with a short stem and a cubelike sponge. These you were supposed to suck without any of the water invading your throat. Thus you could refresh your mouth at the same time as remaining virtuous. This may not sound like an ideal activity for a period lasting several hours for any Oxford graduate but I soon got used to it, and to the different calibers of the fluids that entered my mouth and departed the same way.

It was an interesting guessing game— especially as I had a leaky mouth, so a certain portion of the fluid escaped and created familiar patterns on the invisible bedspread. Besides, this was a way of getting a partial drink. Not perfect, I know, but enough to get me through the night, after which a long day began.

My immediate response was panic or pandemonium. I have already referred to the "Mem . . . Mem . . . Mem." But I grew eventually out of that to a slurred punctuation of such a simple word as scare, advancing to a triumphant statement such as "It's simple." This was so huge a feat on my part that contemplating it made it actually go away, and I could not remember it until someone recovered it for me. How singular to be marooned on an ice floe with a solitary word in my vocabulary, unable to remember it and depending on friends to revive the jubilee of its memory. Double superintendent of my own mouth, with its silent opening, some malignant force took over whenever I tried to formulate a sentence or word and reduced all I said to ashes. For instance, "Ble . . . Ble." Was this some gorgeous prelude to "Bleat, bleat"? Or something of my own devising along the lines of "Bless"? It could mean nothing to anybody, not even the doughtiest researcher, and it reposed ever afterwards in the noxious dictionary that held as well the litany of another aphasic who said "Cash" incessantly, and only that.

To grow, but the outward motion is melismatic, and one has no notion where to grow next. A generous observer might review the situation in these terms: growth has taken place; that's all, otherwise the situation has not changed.

During the first five days of my own case, I was convinced that something was changing between my lower jaw and upper mandible. What came later amounted to a simple relaxation of flesh, implying without demonstrating that one of those days it would go somewhere. For all I knew, it was free to go back, recovering the route it traveled on, or sideways, leaving me with another problem, another outreach of the mouth to be concerned about. Fortunately, this selfless journey from mere outward movement toward mere outward movement that might go somewhere moved into something else. Was this in fact D. W. Griffith's A Birth of a Nation? Or something even more profound, for the force gave every evidence of at last growing into something—maybe only the first letters organized in the wrong order, like slurply for syrupy, but definitely promising.

XVIII

Diane, all through, slept by my side on the matching bed, worrying, rather than sleeping, and supplying me with food that I largely rejected. It could not have been pleasant, sleeping with a man whose insides were oozing, but she did it anyway, little knowing that her life, for at least another month, was going to be the same sort of thing, only much worse, while hoping it might perk up a little and become an object of joy again.

The caregiver in such dramas has a difficult role, verging on the impossible and intolerable, one so often ignored. Bypassed in spite of all one's best efforts and relegated to almost the status of a helping hand at the trough. It is fair to say that a patient remains unconscious through this, as I did; but meanwhile the caregiver has to go on giving almost as if nothing has happened, and the care that's given is a formula for oblivion and madness if pursued too far. "Do you remember," she often asked me, "the Poleskis bringing Melba toast for you to eat?" "No," was my response. "Or how I cuddled you, best as I was able, and the nurses cocked me a cheerful grin as they passed in the night because I was always awake, worrying what would come next?" I often grapple with those days, trying to entice them to do my bidding, but they will not yield up a scintilla of evidence, so I am left with a fantastic illusion of the ghost that walks at midnight and takes no notice of anybody at all.

Such alarms sooner or later bed down in the current of daily life, but they obviously mean more to the caregiver than to the caretaker, and I suppose they must be left at that, unless the suffering gets worse or the operation goes wrong, in which case the caregiver might well be excused for going off her head out of frustration and panic. There is more to be said about this role of caregiver in situations progressively lethal, when mind ceases to be mind and body seems somehow engrossed with itself to the point of no return. Like my friend Floyd Skloot, who while attending to his own problems of brain damage, has on his hands the charming mother who asks repeatedly, "Who is this woman?" (His wife.) And "When are you going to marry her?" umpteen times daily.

You can't write enough about the caretaker in such circumstances, most of it about situations that "normal people" would find incredible. While one person completes the process by which she will never come back from the Herculean efforts her lifelong dedication has driven her to, some other person is marveling at the traditional full stretch she has been called to and just as soon discovers a range of atomic hopelessness that stretches out before her, egging her on to even greater efforts, like some cruelly perverted definition of the promised land beyond the promised version. Either way, the caregiver, at least until he or she becomes the second caregiver in the family, is subjected to extraordinary strain and buffeting that some do not survive but that a goodly number do, and make of their experience in la-la land an ingot harsh and beautiful, like no other in human experience. I am no expert on these ruinous catastrophes, but I know from two or three intimate experiences of the terrible, plus the occasional stroke that gives back a smidgen of what is taken away.

I am beginning to doubt, in Diane's case, if ever our lives will return to normal. She has been interrupted mightily by something that has changed her way of living and it's probably too late to do anything about it. For instance, I no longer haunt the small hours but rise soon after she does for a morning cup of cocoa. According to her, I have a much finer response to trees and flowers than I ever had before. On the other hand, my habitual diet of fishy foods has almost completely been replaced with a diet of mashed potatoes and meat. To while away the time, I have twelve drugs and take enormous pleasure in swimming wherever I can.

Now all was peaceful at last. Above all, no one was coming to visit, which made an enormous change in hospital routine. No one from the imposing mob of overseers, custodians, nurses, doctors, and occasional shepherds whose true responsibility you only guessed at was coming to see us. This meant a huge amount of time that could be spent on just getting extra sleep or on exotic games played with finger painting on windows as well as extra bottles of milk from the dairy.

In short, I was not accustomed to these

modes of living, and I confess that either I felt the need of a nurse's call, or that I had slept enough and needed a new game. Diane, who was present, was busying herself with some of the bureaucratic regulations pertaining to hospitals in heaven or hell and would be back soon, bringing as she always does, vivid reports of life in the outer banks. For the present, all was my almost forgotten foray on the body of Osiris, long gone amid the walking vigilantes, where heaven met hell in a group of underwater nymphs.

You can tell that I was not a soul at ease. I had been cleared by Dr. Ann to go home, though not without several reluctances on her part. I was far from well, and this principally took the form, I was to know from subsequent experience, of not knowing exactly where I was. Was I ensconced on the dresser at home? Or was I still on the Good Ship Lollipop? Was I wondering which of the five or six resident rooms I lived in, or was I wondering at a discarded pile of genes? These dubieties did not reach full range, however, but stayed down among the dead men. All that was missing was an eye or a shoe, but that was sufficient to set my mind rolling between the two fabled worlds—one dead, the other waiting to be born.

One does not go all the way back to Matthew Arnold lightly, but only in matters of need, when his peculiar group of fatal situations, or irrevocable acts of will, seizes one's concentration. Arnold somehow grasped, at least to my taste, the semiblighted condition I was in, and I worried about how long this thing would last and whom it would affect most once I moved into the outside world. For one thing, I had been living an indoor life, when all was extravagant sunshine outside, and this made me more depressed than I would have been in winter. At least I was looking forward to the sun and getting into the pool again.

Most of all, I now realized to my shame and humiliation that the whole startling recognition that my mouth was sealed as by some recondite device of Ali Baba's was bogus and had nothing to do with reality beyond a moment's dalliance. This shock persisted as it would with someone who had staked out his life in intimate detail on that very basis, nominating gristle, fat, tendon as the aspirants to a new dawn.

What I had been so carefully marshaling was no more than a chimera out of intense lying and refusal to give up the ship. I was going to say the rest of me—but I modify that statement. Who knows who is intact anymore? Certainly not I, who have had a kidney stone the size of a lily next to his heart. You learn much from these combinations, and you learn more if you study hard before letting the lily go. Still and all, it would be ever after a shock to find my royals secure as a set of chessmen. Plausibly, some part of me would be bound to malfunction in the near future, but what would any of us care, jumping the life to come, as Macbeth says. We live, most of us, in a world of dumb recalcitrance, saved occasionally by inspired seers.

As I was saying, Diane was back with fresh Roma, which she poured from a new-looking flask that I assumed was a signal of hope for a new beginning. Perhaps this was why the Roma tasted so good: it was as if I had never had Roma before. In its mixture were chicory and, I think, roses, which made the upturn of my spirit even larger. Things were going to be brighter than usual. I could tell from the elated presence of a washerwoman passing by the door who poked her nose in and said good morning. "What's new?" I asked Diane. "Clear to go, except for one final check," she answered, and we both started up as if obeying a signal, then sat down again. "I'd better make a start of getting ready," I told her, and made a perfunctory sweep of my Osiris manuscripts, which I would return to later on by the still light of the moon.

She seemed to doze after finishing our Roma, and I carried my own cup to the brink of the next room, where I set it down again to inspect a telephone that had skipped off its handset. Then I resumed my motion, coffee cup and all, and washed my face and hands. What followed then, just as I finished drying my face, with hands still wet, was like a bolt of beautiful lightning, which seemed to muddle my face in a variety of contortions. For a moment, I felt there had been an electrical surge of the neon lamp or something. But the lamp stayed on, and I realized something had gone wrong with my face, including the head, the mucous membranes, and the jaw that was sealed up beyond all repair, because I tried to speak and call out, without result.

In fact, my head was suffering a kind of migraine attack that pulsed, forgiving, and then returned to the attack. How could such things be? I leveled my face in the mirror and tried the old trick of seeing if the migraine would go away when I blinked, but it stayed the same, and then I felt, as if in latter days' postscript to this abominable happening, an unfamiliar current passing through my right arm. I tried to lift it, and it would not obey me but hung limply there like some trophy of a forgotten war.

How long I remained at the glass, I still do not know, but it could have been several minutes. I still could not believe this thing had happened to me when I was preparing to go, no holds barred. There was nothing for it but to reenter the adjoining room and break the news to Diane that I had had what seemed to be a stroke or a multiple migraine attack. With multiple migraine attacks, we had considerable experience, reducing them to anonymity in twenty minutes or so, but a stroke was a different matter, and I suddenly remembered my previous stroke, twenty years before, when all that was damaged was my left arm, which was restored in three weeks, and my speech, which in fact was restored in twenty minutes. But I was aware of this attack's being what we referred to knowledgeably as the "Big Boy." And it would not be shaken off so easily.

Later it transpired that I had been visited

by something called Broca's aphasia and other
trimmings; the worst of these by far was the absolute
nullity to which they reduced my speaking. For the
first time in my life I was an imaginary toad in a real
garden, quick as ever to spot something incongruous,
but not to report it in the field of action. Diane's
immediate response, lasting only a second, was
to run outside with a look of rueful intentness and
summon the emergency brigade. On her return, she
surveyed the scene of my latest disaster and quickly
appraised the horrible, skewed sinew that distorted
my face from the usual. How she found time to
exorcise this, I do not know, but she focused on the
offending portion a look of such tender regard that
I thought it was the first time she had produced that
particular facial expression.

In a flash it was gone, substituted for by
another in which I thought I heard her murmuring to
herself that he was going down, further than anyone
had gone before him, and those that were anxious
to express final greetings must hurry up. My own
response was less personable, though just as basic. I
have a distinct recollection of seeing my parents for
the last time in one of several natural poses and of
being bewildered by the scene in mind. How could
this be when my father was dead at seventy-five and
my mother at ninety-four? Was I truly going under for
the last time? Going under the hammer, and going
down for the count, and if so, the count of what?

Actually, I felt no more sickly than the low
side of mediocre, which was not bad for someone

going under. Therefore, I almost celebrated: I was not going down at all but merely having a spasm and an underwater visitation from which I would emerge, silent but usual.

Strange to relate, rage formed no part of this response, though I felt in full measure the absurdity of having another stroke, courtesy of Broca or anybody else, and I felt doubly peculiar at having stage-managed the preliminaries. It was not a matter of swapping one for the other, it was a matter of swapping one for none, and this did not exactly take me with the wonder of its devising. I count myself fortunate that the room suddenly became a blur of apparently countervailing ambulance men, all intent on somehow securing the maximum advantage. Surely they were not doing that.

The rest formed a hum in which I lost count of them as they worked their magic, enabling me to sit comfortably and safely while they transported me down the stairs, Diane following with her face a whiter shade of pale than I had ever seen it. Did I imagine it, or was she really looking at the last hours of West, or was she just looking paler than usual, as would have been appropriate?

I seemed destined to always be saying things that became a blur, an even worse blur than before. Which is Chinese for saying that there will always be something left to say. In my recent past, the curious enfilades asleep always left room for another agony beyond the one last envisioned, but not this grim monster, who had wiped out my speech in a single clout and had nothing to do with lightning. At last I surrendered pistol, cutlass, and broadsword, and let the monster have its way with me. My final memory is of being enclosed in a white sheet, whether encasing my head or not I wasn't sure.

XIX

The difference between my own refracted gaze of the
world and Diane's is that she sees the world in all
its detail, squirming into the needlepoint alleyways
that leopards reject, and I look on the offered scene
as a species of broadcloth identified mainly through
its ribbons and tam-o'-shanters. This sharing the
load usually means that between us we cover the
waterfront, missing a few mouse holes and locked
jaws here and there but getting the plurality right.

It may not often happen that our
complementary skills are brought into play
independently, cutting us off in different ways from
the charming scene about us; but when you are
dealing with something that neither of you has ever
seen before—not in bulk, anyway—the situation is
profoundly different.

One way of trying extra hard is to imagine
Diane's dimension of the universe coated in either
black velvet or a blue that no one has reported
outside the province of Baffinland. I imagined Diane
as bringing reports of blancmange, mince pies, jam
tarts, cream pies, chocolate éclairs, Odwalla bars,
chocolate chip cookies, ice cream, and all manner of
other delicacies to the invalid's bed.

However you spell the word invalid, you are
either invalid because not valid or invalided out.
Or you disentangle the least bit of wiry fluff that
has been haunting your tongue for half an hour and
assign it to the unwilling project of the human mess.

These rank as contributions in some way or other, but the assorted confectioneries are too massive to eat, and the strand of hen-pecked fluff is too narrow, which makes them both second-rate substitutes and sees them out. What I'm trying to say, in language ever more oblique, is that the human psyche can sometimes see evidence of what is not present to the senses.

"Bosh," one hears you exclaim, "this man is writing about nothing!" But is he? It could be that he is writing about something somebody said to him after he had regained his senses or that he regained these senses for himself and detected shreds of rabbit fluff here and there. Imagine a man coming round after five days in the human tank that denatures us all and finds no memory worth talking about. I suspected as much from my ten-day immersion in whatever I was immersed in.

I say this in the most tentative manner because there isn't a great deal of difference between what's roiling and not rolling. You could easily miss it for the whole of the ten-day period. Nonetheless, I think it was there for human consumption, and I am content to identify it, if that is not too canonical a word, as a lump of Lot's wife going nowhere or what Samuel Beckett, in one of his wilder notions, identifies as Arsène going the unerring rounds on his bicycle, even when he has nothing to deliver.

Clearly we are dealing with shadowland at its bleakest and should not expect too much. It is not likely to reward us with any vision of something discernible. You always have a chance to say, "I saw nothing" or "I saw something." And it is not enough to say, "I saw Versed or chloroform," because that would generate far too much reportorial weight. To recognize that we are not dealing with much of the known hardly delights anybody, but just imagine how much of the unknown is out there among the dark clusters of stars and the dark matter of which we know nothing. We may think that we are dealing with the nonstop hodgepodge of daily life, but we are also dealing with the opaque mysteries of the universe itself.

Cabbage served twice means death. So says one of the older Greek proverbs, though it goes no further into the lethal lineage of cabbage. I was becoming accustomed to these devil servings, mainly of the mythic cabbage, as distinct from the real one. But how to divest yourself of the mythic one, when the real thing offers itself up? I long ago decided to opt for both, lest I for some reason lose one or the other, whether bull-rushing into a dead end or having the real thing played out on my skull for days.

Was it indeed days? Or merely a squawking interim in the full gamut of time, no more than an hour? I reserved these and other questions for later on when I had got the better of my bearings. For now, there was the serious business of interpreting my condition, as far as decency would allow. First was the matter of my jaw, affixed to my head in the certain manner of a Greek wrestler and extending right through my head with no give in it at all. Some things were happening not for the first time, and I experienced serious reluctance to pursue the matter further. If a locked jaw was any indication, things had already gone from bad to worse and could not be trusted.

I addressed myself next to my temple, which, seeming in no way to have enlarged, felt for the first time brittle and temporary. Could it be that some of it was missing, obliged by some demented operator with a fretsaw to give doughty service? Certainly it didn't feel right and slowly I cruised the surface area, waiting for a mishap or the plain bald gap where something had been and was no longer. So let us say that between one jaw null and void and the other there was a temple that was highly suspicious and would remain so for the duration.

I turned my thought next to the ghostly hand that dangled uselessly at my side, paler than it had been and with an odd look of failure about it that I had not noticed before. Could it have withered during the process? Stranger things have happened to a victim of a stroke. It was the same inert apparatus but somehow more useless, as if it had been ratcheted down a peg or two. In the tremendous lusting ovation of the stroke proper, I rapidly formed an adverse view of my jaw, temple, and hand, wishing them all far away and put to the good uses of someone else who was not too proud of what he brought to the human encounter.

Rapidly turning my attention to my

whereabouts, I very soon wished I had not, for there, as I imagined it, lay a whole suite of uncoordinated rooms, from the one where I had waited in vain for the call to the lecture platform to deliver a talk my mouth would never emit and the second-floor room where I spent one night arguing with two nurses about tax returns I would have to fill out before going anywhere. Also there in this bewildering array were the two redheaded ladies who insisted on bidding me farewell and hoping I would get back to the writing of books very soon.

Most antique of all, there was the strangest impression of noise from the other room, a chipping sound or the recital of a mandolin beautifully played, and several other noises that I could not identify. I stepped across the lintel to check, but both noises had ceased; yet the room had somehow walked with me and the chipping sound and the sound of the mandolin began again. These noises have made a reasonable facsimile of haunting me ever since, so that I often wake at night and go outside, finding the noise has stopped, only to recommence once I step back into the room. I now interpret them as benign, and take them for granted, but all I need is a new noise to get my suspicions up again.

On the whole, the ghostly workplace, as I dub it, though fragmented and in its way supremely desolate, was mine alone, and parts of it began to recede as I became used to my new role of silent artificer. It might be said that my whereabouts remained peculiar, part of a museum set that shuffled according to my mood and would cease this activity when, finally, I was cured and galloped up the hill to where Triphammer crossed onto Texas Lane, and all the joys abounding awaited me.

There was a bewildering assortment of false starts and incomplete sentences for the mind only. I no sooner thought of something to say to myself than I forgot it, and I was lucky to get beyond the second or third imagined word. Of course, no one in his right mind overheard any of this, the dumb speaking to the silent in a reverse image, so no one was upset. But if this happens fifty or sixty times, one wants a little revenge of some sort. Of course, one was in all probability speaking no kind of written English, so this meant that whatever you said was relevant and you could not say anything irrelevant.

I formed the habit of forcing language back on itself, beyond even its failure to communicate anything at all, to see what was there. Language, at least as we know it, had ended, and I was left on countless occasions with something like a white sheet of dental floss or a carnivorous absence. There was nothing beyond. So I cheered myself up by taking as my starting point the notion that all I had to do was pass the zone of no known language and automatically be speaking English once again. These are mental compensations, to be sure, but they serve superbly in times of need. And it isn't a matter of some old Oriental asking another, "What happens when two elephants meet?" The answer is the grass suffers. It is more complicated than that, but not complicatedly so.

So, groggy, weak, and famished, I take my plight on the chin. Milling around me there are all sorts of verbal alternatives both nonsensical and full of meaning, to some of which I have permanent access without speaking. I wonder if one can safely execute a lifetime using the language of dumb show. I know of one woman in New York who has successfully done so for years. It is a matter of the breaks. I would, of course, prefer to speak the English that I know and revere, but I think I can see past gobbledygook to a pure and vivid English, instead of starting every sentence five or six times and writing sentences that lose heart halfway through in a futile clutter of grossly amalgamated syllables.

XX

Always, I have told myself, "Dream the hospital dream." In my case, it was no longer a dream, but a reality where things at first glance didn't have any heft. I was comparing, in this instance, number, time, and intervals with those aforesaid heavy hitters. The strange thing was that my dream of clocks was backwards, but otherwise perfect. My dream of number was also confused; whenever I sought to indicate the time of day, I got it wrong, in maybe three separate ways. It may be said that I was still referring to clocks, but that's all that could be said, and I roamed in a maze of miscalculated times, back-to-front statements, and a profound disinclination to tell right time to anybody. Half the time (no pun) I didn't know whether I was operating on American time or Continental time, and my ventures to tell it right were skewed and loutish. I had also contracted the habit of skipping words in my misjudged sentences, so that mythical persons idly seeking out information found themselves amidst choplogic formulations that only intermittently made sense.

My main related exploit was, in the language of the dumb, to indulge in sequences of utterly incomprehensible pseudo-words. I was saying baffling things and only very occasionally breaking into what I recognized in my delirium as rational speech. But this was a language of silence that now and then promised also to be a language of shadows and dumb show. You cannot ask too much of the babbling dumb, but you must if we are going to get anywhere at all. My habitual pseudo-language of "Pem. Pem. Pem." led nowhere at all, and clearly, when I managed to propel my mouth into the ugly grimace that accompanied these sounds, it would profit from some kind of restoration to the straight and narrow. Occasionally I retained enough motor control to utter nonsense for half an hour, which does not make for an interesting conversation, especially among those who have been accustomed to the highjinks of intellectual performance.

I also had insoluble problems with money. The mere sight of a check bouncing on my horizon gave me the jitters, for I knew full well that I was not equal to the demands of well-aimed and prudently inspected integers, as the prescribed mission required. Several times I attempted to write a check, floundering amid a quagmire of lost vowels, consonants, and little signs I had no comprehension of. I jabbed at the paper only to produce signs where I had not intended them to go, and I reduced my signature to a one-line fiasco. My attempts at penmanship were utterly bizarre and bore no resemblance to a piece of documentary worth. What was to be done with me? The faster I trod into the outside world, be it of checks, time, or beef, I got deeper into the mire and could now be said to be a person of much reduced intelligence, liable for even a police station's remote cell.

This was what I had always dreaded, to

watch my brains slowly decompose until I reached the status of vagrant. How far I was from this final tumult I did not know, but it could not be far away. The question remained of what irked worst, having no sensation in my mouth and being unable to speak the language of man or being deprived of what I must call, in my elegiac way, the means of identification at the humdrum level. I realized that I had already chosen both, for I was dumb as well as inexpert. Surely there must be, lurking somewhere, a third member of this ghoulish trio ready to pounce on what I had left, say my legs and almost salient arm or the other half of my head, or my heart.

So far, no show, but it required only a little intelligence to see that when Drs. Costello and Vohra met for one of their little secret conferences, they were talking about me in the most explicit *sotto voce* way and of what would be done with me when at last I achieved the status of candidate for straightjacket—then onward up to the moon.

Reading, at which I used to be no slouch, gives me the most incredible, disheveled experiences of my print-bound life. Now print jigged toward me, then it hung back. The one part of it that was readable swam backward or forward to render the reading experience at best incomplete or subject to the vilest, maddest vagaries of a proofreader's nightmare. When would it end? The list of possible insults to my body, already some thirty-five pounds lighter than usual, was extending to mop me up, and I could see the day not so distant when West, against all his better judgment in aesthetic affairs, would be lowlier than a bagman. I would become the Ratman of Paris who I invented for a novel!

My sight would get worse, either waning away altogether or producing those scintillates of light that give hope to persons blinded in war and prompt visions of something or other where there is no vision at all. I declined to enter the subject further. Morbidity is usually its own reward, and I could not for the life of me see how things could get better.

Whatever was being done to me behind my back, and under my front, it amazed me that so much attention was being paid to respective parts of my body, so much energy being applied in different ways. To be sure, they had left a great deal out, but they had also left a great deal in. Once again I felt the shady conundrum of life as we know it. First producing a PEM-umbra of what you have and then producing the penumbra of what you have not.

Some kind of trumps, to be sure, but which is which? I never reconciled myself to this idyllic-evil switch, knowing in my heart that I would choose neither and so be left with nothing at all. It was like having to choose between the Hound of the Baskervilles and Jack the Ripper, or some other combination playing into one another's hands. I can never get over the way in which the relevant pieces appropriate to each body come piping through, and I look forward to the day when the miracles of nature, such as stem cells, will officiate as the guardians of our composite bodies. All you would have to do is choose.

XXI

It begins abruptly with a loss in the zone peculiar to Broca's brain. You expect not to be without it. You are. It begins, it goes on, as far as I remember, with a distorted vision stretching on the right side of my face and jaw, a closed space where nothing seems to enter. Whether people find this apparition offensive, I don't know. It felt like I had a weight perched on my brain. And it was no good my saying anything else.

There is more to add to this record. The right side of my ear felt florid, which is to say that a dozen times a day the tympanum would release a florid dissonance that sounded both ten times louder and effectively cut off communication with the trenches. I found this change even more disconcerting than my local outer swelling. It was like being half a man with a nagging habit of probing his ear in full view with the hope of snagging the offending portion. Whatever it was persisted.

Many people would be forgiven, I think, for relegating such an individual to the trash heap of history as someone who had failed and been found wanting or who had achieved a brief prominence and then sunk into the ruck. Who is this, they would utter, who once was so demure and now is so dreadful? Is he human at all with his crossbow eyes and his elephantine stance? Is he deserving of pity or some other outlandish emotion, or should we pass him by? Not exactly an Elephant Man, he goes some small way to being one. What is wrong with him?

We would prefer not to know. Despite whatever agony he feels, we would seek the company of happy, convivial people rather than molder in the invalid's crude animal salon.

I'm proud to relate my legs were almost intact, and I walked on them with brittle ease. No doubt they would break down at the first sound of the trumpet. I walked on them notwithstanding, proud for them because they were proud of me. I would one day soon be deprived of these hostages to fortune, but not yet; I would have many encounters with the toilet basin in my bathroom, placarded black on the front, white on the back.

One nurse, professing to want me to shave, made such a fumble of the toothbrush, razor, hairbrush, lather that she had me in and out of there before I even got to the brush. These encounters in the toilet reminded me of an antique civilization in which nothing was to be complete. Whether your destination was the toilet or the toilette, you always had the sense someone was overseeing you with maximum disapproval and urging you on to complete whatever you were doing before you finished. Here the doings of the Rehab Unit remained in permanent disarray, nurses being the nourishers of life's feast.

I should perhaps explain that for days I was incognizant of what was happening, but I was at one point consigned to the geriatric floor and then as suddenly removed. I was unaware of this shift, or of any other. This made me a nocturnal visitant in both places.

The voices. There is a voice of rhetorical artifice in which I can say just about anything I want without fear of contradiction and another voice that I fear is much of a blur. When I'm on form, the two, while staying separate, overlap.

When I am out of control and should be asleep, there is this out-of-control voice that savages anything I want to say. In almost every circumstance, it provides the wrong words and even exerts a deadly compulsion to say them incessantly. And nothing you can do will correct it, so you might as well shut up shop and go to sleep because you are not communicable on the human level at all. For me there still remains the voice of rhetorical artifice, which enables me to make slow but intelligent conversation with my coevals. This enables those who are lucky enough to be writers to survive. I feel very grateful for it because I don't think it's a unique gift, but it's precious as rubies to me.

Do you see the difference? It's bowlegged but it's legible, whereas the other is mostly nonsense.

The second day in the Rehab Unit I heard the voice of pellucid, articulate reason droning on in the absence of any sound, and I knew at once that I was going to be all right even then, in spite of the evil-seeming things that had been happening to me. I mean that though I hadn't tried to speak yet and the whole world was some kind of abstract fanfare waiting to be fed on or off, I would be all right because I could still think language even though it led to an immensely private universe decorated with the full panoply of speech.

So that side of him remains! I can turn it on whenever I want to speak. It's very eerie. You might say it's almost like having two languages forced upon me: one, the lackadaisical, partly formal voice of the BBC announcer; the other, the rapscallion Calibanesque language of a substitute. No need to say which one I prefer.

Three voices really. One, the faint intellectual voice of the speaker who didn't know whether he existed or not. The second, the somersault-executing virtuoso of my three hours daily, if I'm lucky, of joyous harmony. The third is that speaker you already know too well for his far-flung, defiant nonsense.

XXII

It begins with a rotten start, by which I mean a start that begins well but turns you down partway with an assortment of misnomers. For instance, you can get well away with such references as *moon* but then find it abruptly changing into such a word as *doubloon*. Such swerves are all right for a fit man but, for what I was then, totally unnerving and leading nowhere at all. How would you like it if five times a second you managed to entertain the beginnings of certain thoughts, agreeable at the start, that threw curves at you as soon as you got beyond the first or second word?

Actually I didn't manage to get beyond the first word because what passed for a word in my neck of the woods usually formed three or four. For instance, the sample would run: the letter *I*, the letter *M*, the letters *EJ*, and possibly the letters *AFFB*. With such a workload it would be impossible to complete anything, especially if your mental repertoire extended to a gallimaufry of phonemes such as would render the head of any responsible person insane. It is a far cry from those rounded sentences beginning with "I am" and "He sits" to this kind of thing when no one knows what so volubly someone is trying to say.

It isn't a matter of people not knowing, it's a matter of people knowing you can't hear them in any case: for you are deaf, though not to the spirit ditties of no tone that echo in your ears time and again.

You are deaf in the broadest sense imaginable. You are deaf and they cannot hear you. So what is all the fuss about? They can pass you by without hating you, but fortunately many do not, trying to make sense of your silence. The attempt, of course, is futile and many people rush away from this ignoramus of the woods, thankful they have normal people to return to. I, on the other hand, am left with the illusion of thinking I've communicated something, whereas in all likelihood I've communicated nothing at all and am left with the sad roundelay of all those impossible conversations, firm in my shaky conviction that I've said something useful but increasingly devoid of sense. I suppose this is merely one of the many changes humans may expect in the course of their seventy years from heart attack and stroke and AIDS and tuberculosis. Sooner or later, something attacks everybody, and with that I should rest content, I suppose. One does not change eventualities.

Let me be more specific. A typical member of the tribe called stroke may not remember his own name or the names of his intimates and friends, instead remembering those names as a shadow factory in the wombs of memory but unable to reach the surface of thought. That is why you often see the stroke victim babbling away, attempting to pronounce all the names simultaneously with the word-hoard at his command, but failing dismally. Or consider the predicament of the stroke person who is commanded to raise the right hand and reluctantly raises the left or raises none at all. Consider the fate of someone who is asked to rise from a chair and doesn't know how to do it or who is commanded to rise from his bed of undoing and doesn't know how to do that either. The catalogue of *can't do this* and *can't do that* rises sky high, and I always thought I was profoundly lucky to have two good legs to stride about on, although the rest of me was subject to this or that assortment of ills. Though the rehab facilities are fairly full of people who have lost their hearing despite not losing their wits and vice versa. Or of people who can pucker without being able to swallow and swallow without being able to pucker.

Many a sufferer is subject to clocks seen in reverse or clocks not seen at all or only the right half. Newspapers are alien to most of them, for different reasons, including an inability to read print sequentially and the rival inability to make the print stay in position and not go wobbling about from one corner to the other. Many a poor soul doesn't even know where he is, in China or la-la land, in the eighteenth century or the time of the Schneider Trophy Races of the twenties. Many don't even know which parts of their bodies belong to themselves and which belong to someone else by miraculous sleight of hand. A good many sufferers know no one's name at all, or they try fiendishly to secure it, often going to elaborate lengths to rescue it from some elaborate rodeo game that always produces nothing. How to spell also evades many of them, and a stroke victims' handwriting is fit to drive a supporter of holy penmanship into madness. I once wrote *Poop*,

P-o-o-p, for *Paul* after performing mightily for five minutes on the transliteration, not even noticing the ambiguity of my response. So many stroke victims make a point without getting anywhere at all, piling up errors in language and metatheses. Their end is their undoing.

Most of the stroke victims you will meet will strike you as agitated beings in whom the very slightest setback will produce explosions of rage and shock at the poor innocent in the outside world who has again failed to understand them. These tantrums take many forms, but the most usual, I've found, is a rapidly rising crescendo of abuse when one syllable is pronounced with increasing loudness; for example, PEM. PEM. PEM. PEM. This, of course, is no use to anybody, but it is the best they can do, especially in the early stages, when language seems to enact a signal or a mesmeric function, to the distress of the signaler or mesmerist and to the increasing despair of their company. These outbursts usually grow into something else, either a whirligig of elaborately produced language or even in some cases a return of total aphasia. God knows why. When I graduated from my first weeks in speech school, exchanging the null response of a genuine aphasic for the jabber-jabber of English all around the clock, first words meant nothing. When Diane reported my first sentence to my guide, philosopher, and friend Dr. Ann Costello, in her downtown holy of holies at going-home time, they both burst into tears as if I had quoted Cicero's Latin without any of Cicero's graces.

XXIII

As my plumbing exertions began to mount again,
so did my feeling that once more my head was on
the move: the head that was three-quarters of an
inch beyond my face now seemed to have spread
another quarter of an inch. Could this be true? And
was my head engaged in some creeping transition
to a destiny beyond Mars? Was the quarter inch
to become an inch . . . and so forth until my head
reached the limit of its otherwise inexorable span?
I wish I could be accurate about this, but accuracy
went out the window long ago and all I am left with
is the same old blur.

    I feel a thing and then I don't feel it. Which
is right? Which of the numerous expletives of desire
can fill out the future of an undesirable man? It is not
every day that one is confronted by the changes of
all possibilities, so that for the first time in your life
you don't have to pick sides but accept all conditions
equally as part of the big, golden conundrum life
eventually reduces one to.

    There must be something irresistible, the
first time, about having to make no choices. You can
have it all—and then some. I wonder if it is possible
to live such a life, groping after everything in a
nonstop pandemonium, with everything in reach.
Such elevations are impossible, of course, No one
lives long enough to have a shy at all the possibilities
anyway, and therefore one must inevitably play
favorites with one or the other, hoping to equalize

but never destined to do so.

As I have said, I had that spreading feeling, now a relentless, now a quiet seepage. But there was something there, I could tell that even from the unfurled umbrella of my genes. The rest of my body seemed inert, but that was not to be trusted since my body, as an organism, spelled out its function in several ways. Now rising and falling, then staying still or translating itself wholesale into something it had never been before.

I could not make sense of this mess, though I had tried to in my delirium, always ending up with something that had just happened and was therefore not eligible for praise or that was cheated of happening at the last moment and was therefore not eligible for damnation. I could have spent long years, I fancied, at this fanciful game. But I sensed in some of the activity around me a brewing concern with my wellbeing, or with something much more fatal: a determination to eke me out at a different level, one not as life-giving as before.

I have only the dimmest recollection of having been moved, but there was movement, although some of it came from areas beyond my immediate control. I was being moved gently, firmly, into another world. If truth be known, onto Floor 4 and to the one above it.

Why did this haphazard-seeming shift create such foreboding? I who had no memory to speak of was being appalled by something I had no response to. In the end I let them have their way with me, guiding me wherever they chose and eventually placing me on a rather narrower bed in a ward full of people who seemed to have gone to sleep. Did this prove that I was ultimately awake? The thought crossed my mind that I was in a room full of corpses waiting to be collected by the family or at least carted away unconscious.

I noticed, if such a person as I noticed anything, as I entered the funeral chamber, a little coffee cup commodiously perched on a door frame and wondered what it was doing there and whom it could have helped. I was not to learn until much later, told in confidence by an aide, that this little *pourboire* was the last trump for the dead or near dead, though I could not for the life of me see how anybody at that stage of good-bye could ever need a coffee cup to send him on his way. Which of course fired what was left of my mind with: how did I get here? And what was I doing here? Still vivid in mind, as I pretended to be, and ruddy of countenance.

I made a motion for assistance but no one came and my hand trembled so much at the buzzer that no one had to. Had I been paralyzed? And was this the final reward? Something equally ambivalent and stark was going on in this ward and I was powerless to prevent it. Where had all my friends gone? If this was the last obeisance, surely all my friends would be around me, but they had been banished along with the trim young nurses who scuttled around the floor, not like angels of mercy but like guests of providence.

So I drifted off to sleep for the umpteenth time, heedless of my fate, which a lamentable authority oversaw. I cared not a jot for my fate. I cared no longer to mediate. I was, you might say, in some kind of state of grace and cared no longer which end was up and which was down. How long I stayed in that condition I do not know, but somebody came to visit me, an anonymous doctor and his aide, and sought plausible answers to my enfeebled condition.

I was awakened long before breakfast, the last night nurse's final twist of the knife. I was being wheeled once more past the little symbol of the coffee cup. But to where? I soon found out. I was being restored to my old bed before someone else snagged it, which was surely a mark of status.

Why was I shunted and shifted so? The situation in Bed 11 hadn't changed that much. Dr. Ann and Dr. Vohra reappeared along with two of my friends and I realized, in some degree of apprehension and bewilderment, that Diane was lying beside me. Had she been on the coffee cup array, too? Surely not, as she was wide awake enough although in anxious spirits.

If I thought I was going to be left in peace I was mistaken. Diane produced, I don't know how, foodstuffs of all imaginable kinds, among them many of my favorites. But I was being recruited for several tests and then more tests, in the hope, as I imagined it, that they would find uranium nesting on my lower Alp somewhere. I gave in to them. What else to

do? Diane, at first deterred, opened up her hoard
of goodies and began proffering them now that my
session with the doctors was complete. At least I was
being offered some food. Salmon, sardines, Cheshire
cheese, bacon, and hard-boiled eggs passed my way
only to be rejected. I swallowed one egg. It was not
the time for delicacies.

Besides, I had, with a fleeting portion of my
brain, remembered the caveat against drinking too
thickly.

And besides, the tenor of the afternoon, or
whatever time of day it was, was not submissive
or kind. It was hard Sparta all over again and I had
no idea what season it was. How long had I been
here? And I was not inclined to ask, although several
people, including Diane, responded to my question.
And I as promptly forgot the answer. I was still not
out of Lon Chaney's clutches, though I had inklings
of average cognition. I was still grinning at the faces
at my bedside and was only too aware of the facial
contortions of my friends.

XXIV

Two things half appeared, and I shall rest content in
naming them, although they baffle me exceedingly
in what role they played. I know neither where they
came from or were going, only that, as we moderns
say, they impinged on my awareness.

First was a room—I *think* it was a room—too
small for human consumption, into which I had to
accommodate myself nonetheless. I seem to have
been unpacking books, and I've an abiding sensation
of having left them behind me when I took my leave.
There was a woman visitor who concerned herself
about my eating habits, which were nonexistent. I
was preoccupying myself at the time with some tax
returns, which I couldn't really understand because
the print kept jiggling about.

My brief stay in this phantom chamber
ended when two officious-looking women appeared
and said I would have to go elsewhere or be cast
out into the night. I, being mute, as well as a lot of
other things, spoke not a word to them, and in the
end they went away, returning with a list of all my
possessions, minus my books, and I meekly followed
them to the next destination. Where this special
visitation came from I don't know, but it doesn't
amount to much anyway, and I record it here for its
value in some carriage of the night.

The other apparition took the form of two
oldish ladies who stared at me owlishly while I
picked at my food and were succeeded by a rather

pleasant man who seemed to pride himself on exquisite language. He was always offering to help in some way, as a handmaiden of the male variety. He appeared to be keeping a systematic watch on me although for benign-seeming purposes, and I came even to forming a nickname for him. I called him Mr. Exquisite, to myself, of course. Our meeting terminated abruptly when he announced I was being transferred upstairs to quarters more spacious—and I would next meet him far down the road without his role having changed.

These two incidents recalled my promise at its brightest and promised some kind of future after all, far in advance of my muddled thinking. Truth told, they figured as the best I could do in desperate circumstances. For I hasten to mention them as bright points on my way to perdition and my passage through the dark night of the soul in the upper deck.

These seemingly mediocre, flaccid events contrasted bitterly with my usual fare, which was someone asking how long hummingbirds took to fly to the Caribbean or how many calories Osiris expended on a journey to the Hellespont—both questions of some metaphysical imprudence. Other questions in my sleight-of-hand depravity drew my attention to the gorgeous weather outside and asked what I was doing malingering here. I did not know because three-quarters of the time I was roaming the woods of an almost forgotten homeland, in search of something, I forget what.

Are you forgetting or trying to remember?

What are you doing anyway, dithering about, when we have serious business at hand and no time to waste? This in spite of what seemed like eons of contemplative neglect on their part. Who were these interlopers anyway? Asking me questions about forms of life that I did not know and would have gone to great lengths to quell.

Every time I settled on an idea that would give me courage, it flew from me at top speed and left me floundering in its wake like a rodeo dancer. I could trump up a noun or an adjective, you see, often to an embellished extent, but no sooner had I uttered it, spiritual leper that I was, than it skipped away from me to the paradise of lost birds. It may be that some day all these evanescent ideas will come together, generating beautiful harmonies of well-wrought gold, but for now they serve only to puzzle and confuse me as I try to make my way through the whirligig world of other men.

I had hopes of what-had-happened-to-me being in some way a constructive, although chastening, experience, but it was coming out like nothing of the sort, and I would cheerfully have surrendered these startling, incomplete images to nothing at all.

XXV

In the fuller watches of the night I dreamed I heard
someone say: "They prefer a fuller spalt" or "fuller
splat." By this they meant, I think, a fuller headboard
to the bed. The discussion was all about fitting
headboards and the various types of preference there
could be. I have no idea how human beings could
be so refined about so abstruse a subject, but they
left, on what remained of my brain, an indelible
impression. You know full well how one gains
indelible impressions from silent subjects. I knew
no more than this. It flashed across the sky with an
inaudible report. And then was gone. I imagined
my destiny, if I was to have one, as being denied all
further converse with Falstaff.

Right on top of this interloper from the Dark
Ages of music, or so I presumed, came a flash of
guilt. I had not been sensitive to some presumed
obligation to stand in line and receive a duty. This
meant, in its obscure way, I rather suspected, the
duty to perform a certain function as, say, a lecture.
How this squared interruption got into my mental set
at all baffled me. It was there, though, and would not
go away. I felt I was obligated to do something, and it
was in this service capacity that I would do it. Was it
by any extension of liberal fidelity that I was to take
the smiles of the morning girls literally and respond
to them as if I had really received them? Was this
the dreaded promised finality that sent you off with
a smile or something much worse, the torrential

continuity that plunged you deeper into the mess?

I had the impression that something was expected of me, and that could be a lecture either on friend Schnitzler's works or on the forgotten works of celebrated Dr. Livingston. How could this be? I was dumb and also retarded. What was the point of having me lecture on the arcane mysteries of these gentlemen? Someone clearly wanted me to do it—but how to satisfy them at the same time as discharging my responsibility to the medical program in which I found myself? I worried about this obligation nightly; I was afraid that something grievous might happen to me that had not happened already.

Once again I turned my attention to a lovely girl with flaxen hair, clear dark eyes, and a figure comely and straight. She would deter the malign forces that beset me and maybe even cop me a steady wink. About this time, I realized I was clad in the white hospital clothing of the place I was in and quite unprepared to give a lecture on anything.

I paused to look at something that someone had stuffed into my pocket, which turned out to be, I assumed, the magnitude of tribulations. I recognized by name: Precose, Cozaar, Inderal, and aspirin, among a cloud of celebrated others that I put aside for later. These could keep. The fact of the matter was the half intuition that, after galumphing and gyrating all over the roadway, I was coming around at last— or something close to that. If so, I had no idea how long my ride had been or which area of latitude and longitude I belonged in.

Where was everybody? I was alone in there and had the strangest sensation of being in two places at once. By which I mean I had a brocaded bookcase on my left, and another one six yards to my right, and a cardiac chair facing south, and another one facing the other way. This could not be, and I resolved to investigate the matter further. When I got to grips with it, the brocaded bookcase and the cardiac chair always disappeared. I had not been required to lecture. I had just surfaced, maybe for a fleeting second, before a final descent into the holy of holies. Or was I on my way at last to the surface, where friends would greet me with flowers?

For the first time in what had seemed to pass for my life, I felt I could breathe. No one was there, I confirmed this, and what a charm it was to credit the bright, joyous aroma of that place. Soon, no doubt, it would be overrun by people bearing IV poles, syringes, and sandwiches. That Battle of Hastings all over again. What a battle that had been. Although my fate was far from clear, some signal had gone up about me, no doubt from Dr. Ann, saying that I was at least trustworthy for the next few minutes and was to be allowed some of the delights of human society again.

Although I still felt blurry, it was a kinder blur, and one in which a few objects managed to stay in consort. The best and the brightest may have seemed only the slackest and the dullest; but the whole thing was the beginning of a meal to me.

I was looking for something bell-like or the flavor of an old tobacco, but nothing of that came my way, and I was beginning to lose hope that anything of the kind would come my way. It began when I noticed a noise, somehow brighter and more bountiful than usual, and in my semiconscious way I asked myself if this was an effect of too much light, or was it the light rays bending together to produce an effect denied to most civilized people? In other words, I didn't believe it.

But the noise persisted. And I began to realize, my misshapen nose and my withered arm apart, that things were sounding louder. The sounds, time and again, had me reaching to protect my ears and abandoning the effort halfway. I felt like some poor soul who had been to the plumber to have his ears reamed out and then stood in shock in the street, hearing the first pure noise in ages.

There was another facet to this auditory compulsion. Now and then, as if in some brief reciprocity to my loud noises, the hearing in one ear or the other weakened by a good half. Thus guaranteeing a muffled higher-pitched noise that continued for as little as an hour or as much as two days. The Lord giveth and also taketh away. You cannot have Santa Claus all the time. I was to have an augmented noise backed by a deficient ear and I was once again suspicious of any arrangement that both canceled and restored. Those twin armchairs and other things were taking toll of me once again.

There was another aspect, too, to this

renewed increment of the physical world. I did not notice at first, but several flashings later I remarked that things seemed impossibly brighter, more dazzling. I blinked and recoiled more than I'd ever done in the bright, lofted sunlight of the rehabilitation room. I doubted if this was an overcharge from my eyes, though I would not have put it past them. More things seemed to be touched by daylight. There were just more things waking up. This could be one of the severer diapasons of sunlight; after all, I was only recently in my own kind of murk and was not entitled to swap sunlights.

An even more insidious event took place when Diane, lying opposite me in some comforting position or other that took no account of my moldy face and paralyzed vocal cords, sensed something out of the ordinary: "I felt your eyelashes. They must have grown." "All hail to diabetes," I would have said, if I'd had the vocal power to do so. All was not lost even yet. My eyelashes had grown!

Other strange phenomena followed in the fullness of time. I flinched more when I got into the open vault of Ann Costello and Vohra's external world. It seemed to me that I blinked more and had watery eyes, to boot. When I started eating again, which was not for some time, my taste buds had altered: whereas I used to feast on all kinds of salmon and jars of salmon paste, I now made a fetish of mashed potatoes and the meats. I could imagine that taste-bud changes were temporary, doomed to fall away. I resumed a normal enough diet, but what was I to make of the aversion to fish and the compulsion for meats?

One is at the behest of the machine, and the machine changes its mind more often than we like to think.

How was I to shake myself free of the world in which I was, for all intents and purposes, doomed to stay maimed and have a couple of half-useless arms? Would this situation stay or would its nature change in response to the next aberration of sunlight or the next loud noise from outer space? You see the problem. I was trying to achieve some fixity without surrendering my human disadvantages.

One has heard of all kinds of miracles, upward and downward, and of bewildered humans trying to keep up with those shifts. All I can say is that I was happy to have come through this latest test, if indeed I had, and to be launched on some bright bed of custom-made reciprocity instead of being down in the nether dumps of the planet.

Not much to show for silence, exile, and cunning, with at least half my life blasted out of all recognition, of which I had next to no knowledge at all. And the rest a punished gold of infelicitous combinations in which I seemed to want everything without knowing what everything was.

XXVI

After the first word, if you are lucky, there are others.
Of all those milling around in self-evident joy, it's
hard from my point of view to distinguish them from
each other. The obscure ones seem to take on as
much meaning as the precise ones, and the result
of this mêlée is to half wonder that you will prefer.
You wonder which of all the words current will be
the next ones called into service. I suppose I am
saying that all sentences have a form of sorts, but
not usually as lethal as the asphasiac accountant's,
who was reduced to saying a solitary word several
thousand times a day and no other speech.

I am proposing such speech, something
like what the preparatory schools force on English
schoolchildren almost before they can read. They
have a chance, before correct English has laid
its gravid hands upon them, of learning primitive
English of a high order. They soon lose this
preparatory mode of living and fall into line, most
of them, as the school system takes increasing hold,
but I wonder if a few of them can still respond to the
kind of language that I have in mind.

I have in mind three forms of literatural
language called, respectively, *sophisticated, crude*,
and what I have come to call *surplus* literature,
by which last I intend thoughts that one day will
enter into the grand legion of letters without losing
any of their primal sound. If the idea of a surplus
literature shocks people, it should, because one of

the primary movements in literary discussion favors separating the wheat from the chaff or, as I prefer to call it, the surplus from the achieved. I suppose I am *simply*, with the emphasis on simply, pleading for the recognition of literary language that will appeal to everybody or to someone whose awareness of language has a stunted form, depriving him of language as we know it and forcing him to assemble a counter-movement to it.

How it comes about that, instead of eventuating and then nothing, a sound achieves royal status by gravitating into meaning, I do not really know, but the evidence is there that phonemes do this all of the time. The final huzzah to these miracles would surely be a final sentence so pure and logical and brave that one feels in the presence of an art form that has been unsurpassed. My adventures among languages include many by-blows and many mistakes, but none dearer than the primal, gruff challenges with which I met the first day, when I danced attendance, or nothing at all, hoping for a reprieve. One could not blame them for asking: "Is he always going to be like this?"—warbling the same nonsensical syllable like a racing dog going around and around a circular track.

Another trick of mine was to speak very softly, so that I had no recognizable voice at all, and all the speaking was miserable and a waste of shame. Nobody, even when I got what passed for a voice, could hear me because for some reason I omitted to tell my brain the speaker had a voice. Among my other antics was a tendency to repeat a certain word, as many as ten times, because I could not for the life of me progress beyond it and return the course of the dialogue to its natural voice. How that irritated the kindest of people. Another feature of my speech, almost standard production in the old days, was to forget what a sentence had been in its original form, so that when I got to the middle I had forgotten the ending and so was adrift in each case with a word form that said nothing at all. This happened less frequently the other way around, when I forgot the end, rather than the beginning, but it had the same irritating effect on people and was among the finalists of my last bad habits to be mastered.

If you take another bad habit of using a form of a word, rather than the actual word, you could end up with something like a random *ti, ts, niksn, ti, tkskn*. This was the most irritating habit of the time as it offered no way into even the possibility of language, although for some erudite brains this statement of mine, subjected to a little jumbling, assumed the form of Choctaw.

XXVII

I must report on my detailed physical condition as
best I may, beginning with my mouth. Is this the sign
of something relaxing its grip on me, or a sign of
something increasing its grip until it's strangled me
quite? Once again, the specter had me by the short
hairs. Which way would it go? There was, too, the
incessant dryness of my mouth, which would have
prevented my speaking had I been able to speak
and which I was able to assuage by that good old
champion of the ski lifts, the sponge swab. Was I
dreaming this or was my mouth growing tighter?
Which would have turned my nonspeaking into a
mode of dress not hitherto dreamed of. Even the left
side of my throat seemed a mile away from affection
and I had the dismal reflection that all my body was
soon going to be a silent partner.

Would I one day be able to speak rationally
again? Or would I take station in the miscellany of
cranks who used to infest the railway stations of the
Great Western Railway? To brood on this strange
turn of fate, silencing the man who could never
shut up, seems a spurious offer, like that of the man
who plays one note on his harmonica and calls the
contest a draw.

The strange thing about silence is that it can
go on and on and on, breeding the same taciturnity
without cease. So that all you say resolves down
to one word, no matter what has been the initial
verbal form. Some people may call this the last form

of linguistic masturbation but it is very different, because you always have hopes of turning the page and producing your first well-formed sound. That you find something so banal, exciting, speaks the language of hope, obviously. But you run into statements such as the one in which you are obliged to repeat a word fifty thousand times for it to successfully imprint anew its hold on the language. And this means all of them you have forgotten. Or was the number five *hundred* thousand?

One must look on the bright side and clutch at whatever stays as part of one's dismal armory, whether that number is fifty or five hundred thousand. You savor this small consort of words in full view of the vast sea of language out there among the charcoal seas, knowing you will be defeated in all probability by any schoolboy's notion of completeness. Still, it bears thinking about: the gigantic caravan of all the words in the world versus the few one has of one's own—and some of them mispronounced as well.

There is room, I believe, for all sorts of language. Not only for those thousands of versions of English, but also for the literate formations of people who have been persuaded they are not speaking English at all—and are therefore silenced.

XXVIII

Pride goeth before a fall, or it should, especially
when the candidate for release is a learner getting
ahead of himself. No sane person should have
released me when, confronted by a telephone, I
found its neatly oriented figures meant nothing to
me, which is to say the figure dialed as 1 quickly
became 6, and the usual jumble of wrong numbers
followed. Similarly, when reading a telephone book,
I had the numbing experience of never being able
to find the right number I was looking for—plenty of
wrong numbers to be sure. I, in my bewildered state,
marveled at the telephonic skill required to publish
a telephone book in which all the numbers of my
favorite people had been omitted.

Into the bargain, my sight of things was off
by half an inch or so, especially to the right, so that
a goodly portion of my life was spent in reaching for
the wrong thing or misbalancing the frame—always
the telephone and the receiver but also proffered
food and undesirable drugs. What was worse, I on
numerous occasions found the wrong word, at least
in my muted silence, so that when I tried to say
what I thought, it came out as defective. Imagine the
confusion this could have caused if spoken.

These disasters with the telephone system, to
which we were allowed ready access, provoked (or
would have provoked, if sounded) instant hilarity.
The phoning of almost anybody produced no result,
and there were many incidents along the way. The

time for such as this was far off, anyway, when I would be able to make a calm and collected call to anybody in the human world. I still do not have the hang of it, two months after release, mainly owing to the terrible silence that seizes phone calls from time to time and the wobble of only one key in the mind of someone such as I, who still lacks perfect technique. Most bewildering of all is the moment when the instrument goes dead and the frequently chiding voice of the operator falls dead, too. Then you know what it is like to be lonely in a universe that has not heard of you and goes on about its business day by day.

I wish I could say that telephonic and telegraphic accuracy now and then invades me as I strive to pass muster in this alien element. Were it not for the help of my friends, many a caller would have put the phone down in disgust and vowed to never call again. In another six months, I might have improved, but I still cannot get used to the sound of my vacant voice polluting the airwaves when somebody else might have done better.

Imagine then the recipient of these gladsome gifts being turned out before he is ready, maybe only to get rid of him, into the world of electronics and microcookery. Go figure how long it would take him to singe his finger on the toaster oven or on the television cable. It seemed to me, in rehab, that one was doomed to an infinity of circular evasions.

So it would be no slander to say that we lived in a censored world, from which few were tempted to escape, only the near dead and the dead. It was all for our own best interests, of course. I would even go so far as to say, lives were saved some days by the prudence of the caretakers. Home was its complementary opposite, where visions of home-cooked food brought me the aroma of fried eggs, fried bacon, and fried bread—ah, the paradise that we often failed to pursue.

Halfway in my memory, I recollected something precious: the first book I had remembered since my stroke. This book was Shakespeare's *Macbeth*, a disgraceful yarn of blighted lives and infallible poetry. Why I hit upon this book, of all others, I don't know, but it seemed incredibly dear to me, beyond the actual reach of its concise method. I searched, when I had the opportunity, for a copy in the rudimentary library but found nothing beyond an edition of Jeffrey Farnol's fiction and a mundane-looking book about cooking. I seized the book about cooking, feeling it might become useful someday, and made my way back to my bed, elated that I had somehow cheated the watchdogs that patrolled this section of the anteroom. Unfortunately, I fell asleep after reading the first few pages and then was summoned out to play blow football, an "exercise" that profited me not at all and bored me beyond belief.

It was right to restrain me from all my natural inclinations to head for the open territory, which was only five miles away. I am convinced my life had been preserved several times already and even

was going to be saved again in the long run. The
only issue that haunted me as I progressed in health
from sallow to mediocre was the old question of
my diet. I was losing roughly one pound a day, and
although I had started at 215 pounds when I went
in, I was up to thirty-five pounds lost already and
headed downward fast. Each day the head chef of
the not-so-bad cuisine popped by to see me and
first of all ask whether something had displeased me
with his latest offering. He then asked me if I would
like a special dish, and I responded no, maintaining,
as I thought, my party line, in the face of the
superior blandishments from the staff against eating
unwisely and choking myself to death. He went
away murmuring something about coq au vin, and I
returned to my sniffing of oxygen.

  This merry dance of mine ran the risk of
my being forced to eat food, force-fed, in fact,
and I didn't have long to go before *force majeure*
exercised its despotic control and brought me to
book. At which point I shut off the cinema in my
head, resolving to play that card. And when I came
to it, to look so sniffily at good food was unwise
perhaps, but I had been brainwashed too far for
this local experiment. I wanted to live and not go
tumbling down into the Slough of Despond with my
books, some of them unwritten. If this is a vision
of a glorious future marred, so is it also of a banal
interval cut off. I've hoped for the continually better
and believed I was getting some of it. Although still
unable to speak, I was getting signals from my left

cheek that all was going to be well if I hung on for
a month or three months or a year and did not bitch
about the food.

XXIX

I want to revisit the topic of my arm, lolling in its passive socket. A dollop of an arm, you might call it, with wrist, hand, fingers all useless and with its future all bright before it, with my imagination resurrecting it, stage by stage, into the ziggurat it was once. Reconstruction work has not gone very far since all the attention has been given to my jaw. Obediently the arm rises up when I tow it up with the other hand, and then it crashes down again with a noise like festering eels. To have such an appendage attached to you is no joke. I am right-handed, or I was, and now have to face the workmanlike plight of one who has to begin depending on the other hand. The sooner this arm of mine resorts to its regained status, the sooner I'll be able to get back to writing, a chore and a delight that awaits me several years from now.

Several experts have counseled me on how to begin, reckoning that a man who is mute deserves all the help he can get. First, I am to work on the fingers, three of which look as if they still feel the stirrings of an old clutch, two of which seem to have given up the ghost entirely and emit slight creaking noises when I squeeze my hand under a certain amount of pain. Shall I throw over the whole job and concentrate on getting the left arm in training, or shall I see what the defunct arm will bring me by way of peace offering? My vote goes to the right arm as the one-time tenant of all he surveyed. In addition,

I am slightly fascinated by the idea of a withered arm
rising from the dead and resuming its normal place
in the world.

First I flex the three fingers in which there
is still a sign of life, creaky and arthritic as it is.
Sometimes stroke issues you a little pardon, saying
if you work hard at this a little life will return and off
you go not in the least daunted by the fifty thousand
flexings that you have to do before any of the vital
spark returns. Taunted and daunted, you head for the
last of many roundups, afraid you will lose count in a
short while, and so two fingers as well.

I call this the surplus of the stroke, meaning
that you almost have enough before you begin, and
then you have the stroke proper, which pulverizes
the life out of you, in many instances not to return.
I would have called it excessive, but it goes on and
on, and I wonder in my more cerebral moments if
one day we will have strokes to start with and take
it from there. A monstrous vision to be sure, but
one not so distant from the wilder improvisations of
Joseph Conrad.

XXX

When Carl Sagan told Diane he'd heard that "out of sight, out of mind" translated into Chinese and back again produced "invisible idiot," she laughed, and wouldn't again for a few months.

My own volubilities include the one I am proudest of, and this was "I speak good coffee." This I distinctly remember bracing Diane for, as if I were about to speak one of the noble prose anthems, and ending up speaking these few words instead.

Sometime later, when I was in full flow, I addressed a remark to Diane, referring to a limp she had recently acquired. "Limping little kitten," I said, which pleased her, because she had heard little of that sentimental side of myself for the past months.

I suppose in some way I can be thought lucky: I have a good pair of legs and an almost perfect left arm, which is a hell of a lot better than many patients. I can safely be left alone with my fate, mute and of disheveled intellect (I cannot count, read the telephone book, or sign checks, for instance, because my penmanship wanders all over the place and never comes back to the place it first thought of.) Maybe these minor flaws can be put right one day by an enterprising physician or therapist.

I now return my attention to what happened when the full flagrante of my handicap came to the fore again after being subdued by stroke, unconsciousness, and a big violet rose, shaped like a spider, that hung fast to my gut.

The truth came about in a most unusual and terrifying way when I went next door to wash my face and stared at the face confronting me. As far as I could tell, it was a normal face, perhaps a little paler and thinner than usual. As I stared again, something began to move. Was this an optical illusion sired by long exposure to milk and pure oxygen? The face moved swiftly in a downward direction, dragging with it the corresponding jaw. The jaw collapsed downward until it seemed to set up a new satellite where it should have been, and the teeth went with it. What I had to do in this circumstance was what all recipients of flummery have to do, and that was blink. This did not work. Again I tried to blink and this did not work either. In fact, this seemed to tug my jaw farther than before, past any line decreed by man or beast. So I kept my eyes open as long as I could, hoping to make the jawshifting stop. It did, but leaving me with an inopportune fraction of what my face had been. While attending to my newfound facial hideousness, I noticed something else: my right arm fell uselessly by my side and refused all efforts to pick it up.

The rest is a blur. I felt that each subsequent facial recognition was worsening my appearance. Besides, I couldn't speak to explain. Diane was confronted with the apology for an Elephant Man who was worsening in his condition. The sooner the staff arrived, the better, thus depriving Diane of the opportunity to see any further harm to the neat

outlines of my face. As I said, things became a blur
and I had strange memories of being buried under a
groundsheet, being upchucked again into the mouth
of a raging deluge and then being secreted under
a limelike deluge of earth. What had these to do
with the changing of my face and arm? If nothing,
why has the combination sought me out? One was
surely enough. Now there were three. I had dim,
opaque visions of people bending over me, bending
around me, but they never lasted long enough to
assume cogency. It was like being buried in a world
of fragments, but surely some of me persisted in the
world above long enough to give me harness on
identity, but that, too, in all probability had changed
and was now the face of Shelley's Ozymandias or
amounted to a rift of clouds. This at least could be
said for phantoms: They were supplying me with
rich, disordered fragments of a world I thought I
knew, but in each case I found I was wrong; each
shape was the beginning shape of a shape I thought
I knew but then had mutated into a bolus indivisible
and strange that I have never seen before and in all
probability would never see again. My sequestered
life was becoming a disrupted scherzo.

What was uncanny about the arm, in all its
grandeur, was the way it seemed to collapse upon
itself, falling in sequence from fingers, knuckles,
wrist, and the body of the arm, to rest in a not-
unlikable pirouette by my armpit. I could even for
a few seconds hold it out and have it obey some as
yet unwritten law of gravity and perch there on a

pilgrimage to the Tudor forts. Of course it collapsed as soon as viewed.

I quite a few times thought that an interesting art form could be made by having the left arm ascend and collapse, and the right arm ascend only a few seconds after it and refuse to collapse. I kept all such thoughts to myself until now, convinced that such rumors distributed along the Rialto might dissuade some clever person from abandoning his lifetime's deformity. But I'm not so sure now, feeling that any attempt at wholeness is worthwhile, not least to the persons with this or that deficiency to their name. I leave it to you, the experienced connoisseurs of human frailty, to set the matter right.

This almost jealous regard for the finer elements of one's being or for the cruder elements will strike some of us as self-indulgent. Tell that to the young woman who was carried into the county hospital, eighteen, if a day, with a severe stroke and the need for stent placement by the physician. Tell that to the sixty-year-old psychiatrist who had a stroke, also severe, which restricted his walking to fifteen feet and silenced him for the near and possibly permanent future. Also tell that to the German who took three swings at a nurse before consenting to have treatment for his stroke and was the next day removed without more ado by his family. These people are not concerned with the degree of destitution the stroke has imposed upon them. Only mild to moderate bone pain.

XXXI

One can easily and pleasurably be consumed by an organ, as was the neuro-anatomist Alf Brodal by the hippocampus in 1947. Such absorbing labor can take year upon year out of a life, and I don't have that in mind at all. Instead, for a change, I choose to observe the wonderful behavior of tissue or blood about me, noting second by second the regularity and consistency of its metronome-like beat. Although I do not pretend to be any kind of authority, I marvel at the steady way the organism keeps things going, beating and measuring till the cows come home.

It isn't a far reach to blood, and it is more obvious and flagrant an item, but it is possible to see them dancing together in elegant concert as if the whole universe depended on their unanimity or fidelity. And when I say these things, I mean fidelity to us, a living species that nonetheless would go their own ways to a quite different destiny if their mechanism suddenly failed. I remember a piece of jargon from my days in the air force that described the human condition as "flapless," by which we meant not easily perturbed. I can see it now, the bare splendor of tissue, blood, and saliva, with blood for the uppermost, and one day caving in, as it must: the blood just follows its track in another direction, and the three tissues fade away into the forest dim until yet another pathologist heaves into view.

"No trouble at all," say the organs and tissues. Just doing what comes naturally. And what

delights me, when I am so disposed, is the way
the human organism keeps going much the larger
part of it, when single things like the jawbone
may be breaking down. One does not have to be
a neuroscientist to single out these relationships,
multiple or singly, only an observant one. They are
part of life's unconscious flow to a very narrow
destination and will keep going until time cries,
"Stop!" You would think, therefore, that on the one
side you have an organ that's malfunctioning and,
on the other side, all the rest chiming in perfect
order. But reality is not like that at all, and we resent
anything, even in the slightest, that does not do its
duty. I try nonetheless to heap the good on the bad,
saying it's only the jawbone of a pixilated ass and
shouldn't be made too much of.

This bright moment of virtual seizure
lasts only five minutes, and then I am back at the
grumbling game, arguing why the offending organ
does not fall into place with the rest. You can't win
them all. Another way of gleaning some comfort
from natural surroundings is to take a flower or
natural perfume, if you happen to have either on the
premises, and inhale it deeply; some recently arrived
flower child will have the one, and some recently
arrived lady still caparisoned in patchouli or eau de
cologne will have the other.

"Oh," you can say to the flowers, real and
artificial, "You smell more than life itself is worth."
Or going further afield and making your apt oblation
felt where it counts, "What a nice structure for a

harebell! And you, beautiful crocus, spread-out winter dares you to get no nearer!" Or you address the nasturtium: "You valiant creature with sails like a yacht in autumn, do you never get weary of crowding out the crocus?" Such fanciful eloquence is not to everybody's taste, but do I resort to it occasionally when I run out of steam and patience with the lackeys that support the various varieties of our sickness.

For this is a sick man's book, to be sure, and though not exactly bursting, got me out among the hay fields and the oats. I sometimes get the yearning to be merely out somewhere, commanded to return in fifteen minutes by the stern voice of the day nurse. Anywhere will do, even one of the rundown buildings favored by my prose friend William Gass, who adores nothing more than a brisk trot through the architecture of a forgotten world that even in its chains and bottles is eager for a second round. That, you see, is one way of incorporating a friend into an area where he had half expected to be, since he was elected recently to the pacemaker club just before the celebration of his eightieth birthday.

I have spoken little of anger in this book. This does not mean that I have not wasted days fuming and stewing with a longing to go home, even though my condition marked me as unfit. There are times, though, when the sheer fury at some nurse's refusal to make up a bed or to detach a Foley makes the pot boil over—the innocent catch it in the mouth. Or when some hireling donates the entirety of the blackboard to a hodgepodge of ridiculous word games, building games, and board games, interspersed with sessions of walking or calisthenics.

Though, to tell the truth, I, in my dumb, silent state, was most offended, as I have already said, by being awakened at four in the morning and left to my own devices until breakfast was served at nine. Tethered by my two-inch rope as before and commanded not to use it, unless for the most serious of ablutional occasions, I think this kind of frustration builds, developing into a final yell and sundry, whether the last kick of the knife is inspired by a dimwit of a camp counselor or by an aide who has an appointment with you for playing with the pretty blocks.

I know of some equable souls who take all this in their stride, who confront the worst excesses of the Gauleiter brigade in their stride, wanting nothing, holding urine long past bursting point, and not even complaining when they're denied dinner. But I am not one of those eager beavers who will swap the portrait of Rilke or Stevens for a mess of pottage. In the circumstances, I seek to fix my gaze, if she's there, on the most beautiful girl in the world or, in the outside world, the most attractive nurse available, feeling that most human events ultimately even out, and if you wait long enough, three kings of Orient will come riding on your breakfast tray to announce that you will not be required for further exploratory surgery after all and that you have a clear bill of health to go home at once, where someone is waiting for you with open arms.

Perchance to dream. It does not happen very often in a place like this, with measurements, scales, and glucometers to burn. You are kept on your toes to pass muster. I myself call it a hospital, attentive to drugs but with people unpalatably harsh, with, let's face it, some male and female nurses whose pride in their profession wins them kudos daily and without whom life for most of us would be bleak and unrewarding.

The other day, a distinguished scientist came to see me and in the course of a very, very thorough examination of a point I myself would not have asked about, asked me to sing more, as it did something beneficial to the throat, and we are always looking for things beneficial to the throat. Then he asked me whether I sat in the same position all the time, he having noticed that I shielded my right arm with my left when sitting in repose.

Small wonder that I did so, having, as I thought of it, brought up my right arm to be, at first, limply erect, then firm as a grenadier guardsman, and finally to exercise the last two remaining fingers so they made a quintet when assembled for view. I was not aware of doing this except when in the pool I clenched and unclenched my fingers to make them pliable. It sometimes hurt. What a good idea he had, because there was always something about these two fingers, nesting where they lay like two crippled birds. They needed someone to still look after them, maybe forever.

This observant technique of his gave me a new attitude toward my fingers and, once having started the idea, it would be difficult to lose it until I had achieved mastery of all five. From now on I would nestle my two weak fingers in the pool, half protecting them, and half stimulating them to Olympic efforts. But I am getting ahead of myself, although the very thought of it gives me positive pause and a smidgen of light where there was none before.

XXXII

What followed was one of the most undervalued
events, a mild surprise: part of the jaw seemed to
offer a diffident movement upward, not even to
the practiced eye a movement, rather something
approaching a quiver that ended as soon as begun.
I realize this strikes many as something fanciful on
my part, but you call them like you see them, and
this even on the Richter scale merited at least a six-
thousandth of a millimeter.

Dare I say the jaw, or some part of it at least,
was on the move? Which way, up and down or to
either side, was unknowable within the range of
minute gradations. A humorist might say that this was
one of the eternal mix master's final potions, but an
absolutist might refer you to something larger, such
as a spider's dancing feet. I myself multiplied the
result a million times, talking it up instantly beyond
the snows and the earthquakes. This dapper move of
mine was intended to forestall other moves on the
part of my jaw, but of course it didn't, although I had,
as fleeting opportunists of the wildest will can vouch,
a single slant instance when all appeared to me in
place and I saw myself arguing agreeably among my
confrères something or other, and jubilantly so. Then
it was back to the millionth of jaw movement, and
the minute, Sisyphean climb to greatness. I was glad,
and this jaw had made it so.

I would be remiss if I did not pay tribute to
the other parts of my ailing body that played a part

in this movement of the third floor back, such as the cheek, which blew a mite outward as if inspired by a procreant wind, and similarly the throat, blowing a bubble internally to see what effect it had. I have no doubt that the effluvia itself played some part, dragging some portion of itself to a place it had never been before, then dragging it back, just for the sake of exercise. These are the rejoicings of a man who, feeling taxed beyond belief, has finally crossed into the Promised Land by way of Sinai and looks to a superior fate from now on. Little infinitesimals that border the range of thought, hardly perceptible to the outside world but rare as stem cells or radium to the battered observer.

Of course, to the practiced observer, this was all dumb show, a jumble of muddling cells on the verge of a nervous breakdown and liable to vanish thereafter, having done their dastardly work. In my imagination I affixed a sign reading: ABANDON HOPE ALL THOSE WHO ENTER HERE, BECAUSE YOU WILL BE DISAPPOINTED. Even your saliva will not meet your needs, and all will terminate in a mad shimmy toward the frontier of light, never to return. The only survivors will be those who have nothing to gain and so accommodate their striving to their needs, glad of a minimal portion of attention from the gladsome hand that selects so few for treatment.

During my first periods of awakening, I had to go downstairs for treatment. This involved stripping down for something called Mother MaGee's Irish Ranchero, which obliged the lucky recipient of these forces to first entomb his limbs in a pressure-measuring device in order to produce an astonishing result, astonishing anyway to Mother MaGee, who I personally suspected of being a Nazi spy from a distant age. After this, similar tests were conducted on the head and the torso, requiring the same kind of pressure and the same kind of result. Mother MaGee kept all the machine's findings to herself, so I promoted her to the CIA in hopes of landing her an appointment farther up the scale when all was revealed. These things accomplished, Mother MaGee, with an Irish tap on the buttocks, which missed, said I was free to go, and the waiting aide who had been there all along wheeled me into my wheelchair once again and carted me back. "Isn't she an amazing woman?" he said. "She came from Latin America." And that was all he was prepared to say.

Safe again in my bower, I reviewed the situation and found it grossly enigmatic. What was she doing in a place as august as this, with indefinable spurious credentials? Surely we weren't to be classified on the strength of Mother MaGee's wild Irish ways, whatever malfunction of this or that limb we boasted. I never, even months later, cracked the nut of Mother MaGee, although I did hear on the grapevine that she had returned to Latin America with her boatload of bounty intact. And I still have hopes of establishing, one of these days, the whys and wherefores of Mother MaGee and her Irish tempest.

I was also called down below, in the form

of a service to Mammon that was rapidly becoming second nature, to be x-rayed, a gesture that was several times repeated. During it I felt, as well as feeling dumb, of course, as I was for Mother MaGee, that, however they positioned me for some of the peculiar rites the machine required, I was lighter than air. Certainly not pulling my own weight, as they say, and liable to fly away at the merest touch of a hot rod. This obsessional positioning of the human victim seemed to give the x-ray technicians a lot of fun, even sexual, and I thought it only required the offending part to hit just the very spot of positioning required to set the whole posse of them in a true dervish's delight.

Put another way, these technicians were looking for another world to sport about in and, once they had found it, would be likely to disappear from view. And the sooner the better, as I recalled bouts of impatient adjusting and funereal tickling that accompanied each of the several performances. Certainly, since I had come on these visitations to the terrain of Mother MaGee and the x-ray boys, with calisthenics soon on the way, I had begun to tire of their antics and wished for them a head-in-clouds disappearance. But life was certainly warming up, as even these febrile exercises revealed.

I have omitted the role of the doctors in these painstaking and protracted performances. There must have been half a dozen practicing this or that black art on my body simultaneously. Some were cold and laconic. More than a few were cheerful and bumptious. And some were consistently charming, arriving with apologies for sticking me yet again in either arm for their ritual booty and apologizing for the tricky machines they sometimes had to operate to get results.

As I remembered it, and remembering here means a five-day blank impaled on a universal dumbness, I was fed initially three times a day times thirteen portions, the worst one by far in the morning, with a taste like brackish pond water mixed with cantaloupe, the second one almost tolerable but not quite, reeking of brackish sulfur, and the third a state of sublimated raspberries that, according to your state of being at the moment, sometimes tasted almost pleasant but at other times rather not.

These things they fed me with, almost three gulps a feeding, occasionally pummeling my tummy and saying, "You are still not eating." "I can't," I said, and left them to speculate why. I soon learned to subjugate the worst of them to apparitional status, the best of them to a glorious room in which they saved me from all further ills by resorting to a nonstop deluge of advanced chemicals. Some of them, never the bad ones, asked about my condition, even inquiring after my slow-to-move jaw and occasionally disturbing Diane. I noticed with increasing alarm the extent to which a frequently visiting person could be siphoned off in a wake, and thence to a phantom fun-loving hooligan.

The doctors attending my case were a mixed bunch, but four or five of them were as good as I had seen and made every effort to see me whole again and sent off home. I would like to praise the often not-noticed nurses who came in and, not without a certain pleasure, clipped my fingernails, toenails, and even on one solitary occasion my nostril hairs, leaving me pomaded and aromatic, even as I slept. These little services made real an experience that only too readily bombed off into the wild and grotesque, leaving me with nothing to hold on to.

These little clips shored me against my ruin and, when things started to get fractionally better, became a basis for devout recognition. Clipping the toenails of scores of patients demanded some fortitude, of course, and I marveled at the accuracy of the treatment. No blood was spilled that I saw, and no human being was sent yelping against the brace that held him in. If those nurses who had declined to make beds had joined hands with the ones who did the clipping, there would doubtless be much bloodletting and shrieks of pain as a result.

XXXIII

Time waits for no man except the race of scribblers,
for whom it dawdles with scant regard. My own
indulgence began the day I sensed something
of a tinge in the makeup of the jaw. It was as if
some musculature had lightened in tone and had
decided to go on a slightly different route from the
one prescribed for it. Or, to take the phenomenon
another way, it was as if a tiger resting on a nest of
eggs had spared just one.

There was something almost mystical about
it, whether tiger or any other foreign body. And it
felt like something had changed color, only very
slightly, not enough to distract one's gaze. Or it felt
like a cloud coming free in the empyrean, but only
fractionally so. It centered on the very top of the jaw,
and not, as some would expect, on the fringes or
the fringe. To tell the truth, I had the distinct sense
something had given way or slacked off, maybe only
a little bit but enough to make the heart rejoice at
something unexpected.

I almost at once multiplied the result by
thousands upon thousands of cells, styling myself
with the brand-new jaw and little twinkling teeth.
With this I could go out and mash an Easter egg in
seconds. The main thing, as I see it, was to keep
up the average of one or two improvements a day
until I had what the Jews call a *minyan*. This course,
developed over a month or a year, could only lead to
good and might bring with it a hula dance of sheer

elastic mobility.

I was resistant as well, not wanting to overstep myself but never wanting to go a day without any noticeable improvement in the matrix. What was important was to maintain a decent average score that one day would terminate in a perfect jaw with nothing to add. It may sound preposterous to find someone welcoming his jaw back to the family after a sudden savage impulse had negated it, but my role was to let things ride until they got better.

Of course, things may not have got better no matter how long you waited, but that is the epic chance you take in almost all of life's heroic adventures. So long as that little embrasure in the wall kept on with its residual seeping, I was mollified. But then, you are entitled to lose or gain a modicum of faith so long as you maintain it as an open question: no cocoon is a chrysalis and no monkey is a simian.

There was a noise that felt like the faintest frying of an egg, and I sensed this was the prelude to my day of glory. Other times, though, either the egg was silent or seemed to be going backward into some hitherto undiscovered wall of darkness. In fact, you could not count on the crescent cells going one way or the other. It was a question of adaptability, letting the thing ride or come to a standstill without worrying about it, because it was plain to see it was the master of all things without end.

So you see me carefully hedging bets as I

prepared for my day, either being wheeled off for
another round of speech therapy or being elongated
to another session of calisthenics with the idiot
laboratory of plastic tools. You learned to take the
rough with the smooth and to appreciate lunchtime
and dinner, even if you did not partake of the fare.
You nibbled, it is true, a pancake there and even
sipped a mug of woefully thickened Ensure, designed
to put weight on your frame, even though you failed
to.

Life was, as they say, looking up just a little
bit. No cigar and no chance of a ritually exact
celebration. I can't resist the feeling that if we had
been asked to do twice as much speech therapy,
instead of calisthenics, we would have been better
off and the sooner would have arrived at its promised
destination. Playing with a ball or identifying paper
mascots on the wall is not my idea of vigorous
therapy. Which is to say, we would all have been
better pursuing a course of busy language studies.

The reader may detect an increasing
confidence with the language, though no
recognizable words were coming out; I did manage
to now and then make a noise like a war whoop,
a sizzling sound like the one in the matrix itself,
and two or three childish little chirrups that would
not have graced a cuckoo. Not bad for a beginner,
would you say? The reader will have noticed, too, my
hostility to the phys ed exercises we were obliged
to practice, confidence that grew with my old
profession of teaching.

I was beginning to invent novel ways of enlivening the class and I didn't care who knew it. Actually, though, I was perforce dumb as almost at birth, and I shared Diane's impatience with my slowness in language studies. I still could produce hardly a word, although I had learned that a wordless greeting is worth many smiles and an actual word is a blessing in disguise. Soon, we both hoped, there would be the occasion of the first word. For now, there would be the approach to that blissful state and, on my part, a diligent effort to make the beast obey.

Almost daily I was escorted down the aisle of the slow-motion wheelchair to luxuriate in a bath, and it all would have been like some Roman pleasure dome had it not been for the regularly glowering countenance of my keeper, who would favor me with the tune of "Jesus loves me this I know, for the Bible tells me so," there and back and during. This oaf, whose breakfast-time greeting was a dismal scowl, accompanied by his only other piece of prose, "Here's yours," dominated the scene. He must have had some in, somewhere, for he was a hopeless wastrel and would have been better off in Dickens's Dotheboys hall.

Being invited to take a shower by this creature struck me as the best and worst of ills, for he contrived to produce, even when his face was in repose, the same evil expression. In a way I was glad when the shower was over and I was escorted back with a warning not to tinker with the alarm.

Slowly my legs improved. My limbs felt more fibrous and my inert arm was now going up for the briefest time and my left arm was ascending for the briefest time before collapsing in an abject heap above my feet. My body was waking up, although in ill-coordinated, healthy jerks, and this led to my serenading it when it was at its most relaxed and inert, the melody something like, "Sweet body, with its aspiration to almost nothing, I will stand by you." Not much of an aubade for a whole body, but enough of one to revivify the mechanism for another five minutes.

I hadn't been on such good terms with my body since my cricketing days and the sensation was intoxicating, with its suggestion of crispy bacon fried just right, bald effigies of crocuses and dahlias in the sunlight far beyond the planetary boundary, and what I found to be the signature of the sun, all cupric gold and regular in its habits.

XXXIV

Monkeying around with a piece of ham (shall I
eat it or not?), I wondered why the reputable souls
who read a blood sugar bother to do it at all, finally
rejecting the piece of ham and turning my attention
to how the inside of my mouth felt as it began to
stretch. First it felt like it was too much in there, all at
once, and could have done with the excess removed
and transferred out somewhere. Then it felt normal
again, and I felt unjust for having chided it so. What
was happening in there was a trick of the trade,
pulsing with a mouth, this way and that, to the end
of time.

Reaching up to my next station I felt a rim
that did not have a partner on the other side of my
mouth. That must have meant something, a prime
inflection or a brush-toting God who put it there
in the first place. I didn't know, and certainly it
was extra baggage that I did not need. But was it a
scandalous piece of my overdeveloped mouth or an
uneven pelmet designed especially for me?

My faith in the unseen matched my trust in
the usual. I was batting both ways, both before and
behind, to catch the uneven world at a swipe. Either
way, I recognized that old favorite of mine called the
double banger. I was caught up again in the world of
too much versus too little and wanted to have it both
ways: let's leave that to its own devices. Either way,
the equation doubled back on itself, in each case
requiring of me a gesture of desperate levity, a trick

associated with something called swabs.

With this you slaked the thirst off your mouth, thrusting in between, as best you could, gum and teeth. The resulting easement could not have lasted above a minute, but it certainly met the case of the barren mouth, offering it a moment's relaxation amid the forest of dryness that you associated it with. Maybe someone should invent a long-term drink, ideal for up to half an hour of fluid refreshment. Certainly a minute was too short, especially when you had a mouth whose raging constant dryness drove you to emitting a substitute sound that otherwise should have been a letter.

No one had yet done this, so I assumed that its invention would be a drag on the market and of no use except to somebody like me whose career had wandered from the straight and narrow to the inferno's regions where the heart craved moisture. How odd it was to find myself strutting the same dull innuendo. There was not enough water to feed an ant, which is why, whenever I was summoned down to occupational therapy, I was to be caught licking my chops at regular intervals, whether equipped with a swab or not.

It could not have been a labor of love to find an old gent slopping his chops before your face and furtively trying to conceal emotion in a handkerchief. I've heard tell of incidents such as this, but only at secondhand, and I suppose that even the loutish subservient handkerchief would elect to bring a handkerchief to hide behind. All this, and with all the many futile attempts to produce an English saying from an otherwise ribald litany, the words never got through, sometimes taking flight from a cacophony of uncouth-sounding jabber or intending to convey the sweetest tone of language—"Ha" or "Ah"—that had ever been heard.

This was a kind of dreamland of the upper senses, with people who had advanced beyond stage one, muteness, without having advanced to stage two, reason. I don't know how many such creatures there have been, but in my darkest hours I hear them all in a mad, terrible crescendo, snapping at one another in a desperate attempt to make language that someone understood but only succeeding in driving the world crazy with their babble.

Stage three was a long way off and would forever be. I imagined myself at ninety or a hundred, extorting the same sounds as before, only amplifying their noise and determination: "Ah" and "Ha." Wilder things have happened, but not to this slave. The language of romantic longing seemed a long way off, and my dream of confronting this or that custodian of mouths was paralyzed between "Hey," at ninety and "you" at a hundred. The ones who escaped this mad transit of brilliance departed to Shangri-la and were never heard from again.

I wondered if the same fate would befall me or if I would stand out as one of the last renegades of the system, who had somehow managed to last until the end of time, merely by pronouncing his two syllables with demure regard. How much longer would I have to endure the languageless wasteland of two syllables— ten or twenty years? If there was some fleeting generosity in the world, envisaging success in a year's time, I would buy it, but there seemed no way out of this barren portcullis of words. How soon would the charming invitation to the waltz take, with me for the first time addressing my partner with fluent melody and no mistakes?

I preface this sketchy view of the language of the well-educated dumb-show recital with a brief intimation of how one fares at the telephone, given the right opportunity. The diligent pursuer of numbers will find after many alarms and mistakes an X staring him in the face. This symbol, according to the telephone itself, is to be used for calling the operator only, which leaves the telephone without a symbol for O. Many's the time I have looked for O and, not finding it, abandoned the attempt. It may seem obstinate of me to let X do for zero, but I am not enough of an antique Roman for that. I just do not believe it and, guided by the telephone itself, which has to educate some of us out of our Roman ways, suspect the telephone company of working a miracle against us in the lower order of mutes.

Things sped up. Time's tinny trumpet achieved a few plangent notes and swiftly swallowed them up. Anhedonia cracked in. There was a quickening in the afternoon as my verbal attempts continued. I had graduated, by now, from "Mem. Mem. Mem," which was nearly language, to "Men. Men. Men,""which was language right and proper.

There followed on these nonsensical exaggerations not exactly a host of words but a series of reminders. "No" would not shake the timbers of an old man's dream, but "It's simple, stupid," might disturb any person looking for a topic.

To have been responsible for such elocution was amazing. With me, traipsing though the thicket of language to achieve a final effect of racy jingoism was capital. How exactly I did it would remain a mystery, but I suppose it could be said that I had been preparing for several months to combine phonemes and vowels to just such an extent. Such an outlandish phrase may not come my way again (it had better not), but for the moment it was a triumph of self-mastery and ironic verbal control. Crows have shrieked nobler orisons than that one.

My next venture was of the series that I referred to as semiautomatic, faintly offending the stories of H. G. Wells in the use of parrot language. I said "invisible idiot," a triumph of a different kind, calculated to bring into play complexities of thought beyond the average man and certainly beyond the kind of man we had on the premises in that drab quasi-military room. I must confess, of all my phrases, this was the one that lingered longest, maybe because it echoed a fine mot of a Chinese scientist who once upon a time foxed the wits of Peking with a similar saying. If he continues to outwit them now, good Chinese luck to him. We have moved on.

My major effort in this mode was a phrase

that had been haunting me for at least a month, but
I couldn't get it out. On a triumphant note I said
to all and sundry, "I speak good coffee," a passing
reference to my old skills as the coffee maker, now
lost in the sands of time along with Ozymandias.
I must have used it, once having explored its
accreditation with humbling nervousness, several
times until I had it right. First stumbling all about
the phrase—it was my first four-word exploit—then
stumbling further as I worked each word in turn
through the mazes of my corrupt language.

I knew Diane would come within moments
and I once again rehearsed the phrase, all-complete,
as the French say, pending her arrival. When she
arrived, I thought, "Boy, do I have a surprise for
you!" She glowed with a nervous sheen, and I began
speaking as slowly as common sense would permit
until I had it all there; four words masquerading
as four postage stamps a million miles apart, for
it seemed that long to get it out. Hearing this, the
highly imaginative woman said, "What? Say again,
please." I did, advancing my individual words off
the scale of temerity until I had nothing more to say
and closed my mouth. Now she was speechless, for
to her I had turned the corner from my putative best
and my most lyrical utterance to something that had
structure and a name. I had, as it were, declared war
by making that very pronouncement on all the other
coffee makers in the world, and I was not about
to retreat from my position until I gained a phrase
comparable in wit and worldliness.

The contrast between my lame tussle with my mouth and, lower down, its jaw and other features, readied me for my outright war with the other consonants and vowels. I was still speaking with contorted mouth (it still had not regained any semblance of its former shape). My teeth were somehow still out of joint, and my need for little, a drink of cold water, kept me mighty occupied, bringing to my mouth every ten seconds the cup that refreshed. I had developed, it seemed, a shelf within my mouth to accommodate the bulge of its outward movement, and this was surely not part of the eternal plan.

It got in the way of my finest offerings and I could only make sense of the lines I was trying to say by catching my mouth off guard and so skewing the pronunciation of the word. Equipped with these difficulties, or in spite of them, I was not a free agent. I was a handicapped one, lured by some architectonic glitch into a verbal motion I could never repeat to my satisfaction, and I never knew where the experiment would end, leaving me half stranded between polyglot and uniglot for all time. I should have been grateful for anything I got, however infinitesimal, but I wasn't, feeling my way up the rope ladder of language, bit by bit, until with a clarion call, I reached the top.

Seen from a distance, this motion of my mouth from norm to stroke, and then a series of hesitant glances toward a second norm, would be trivial. Close up, however, it was excruciatingly slow, buoyed up by my recent prowess in language. Prowess, I call it, but it was a poor journey to travel along the circumference of my mouth to rest, glowing with pride, on such a wasted concept as "I speak good coffee." The relegation implied, for one who used to be a master of language, had already passed the stage of humiliation and found a new outlet in the high jinks of a joker's trade.

The weird thing was that I was still hearing the three voices of before: first, the manicured tones of the BBC announcer, droning away to the heart's perfection; then the comparable but at the same time very different American-toned language of everyday use, which I preferred, although my periods of endurance totaled no more than three hours; and finally, the gibberish I spoke for the rest of the time, twenty-one hours minus eight hours sleep, in which I spoke, if that, with hectic Calibanesque brio, which amounted to only a dozen phrases for the whole evening's performance.

The point was to cram as much orthodox wordplay into the three hours allotted before sundowning, as the argot has it. And, when in difficulty, to enlist the aid of the BBC man speaking continually to my inner ear, Lord knows why, who was often capable of finding the right word for one in extremis. I realize this must seem bizarre to some who have not known the ways of stroke, especially those associated with Broca's little ferret hole. This chap claims to have three voices speaking to him—a BBC voice, an orthodox voice, and gibberish? Does this mean three voices speaking simultaneously? No. They speak in turn. And two of them in complete sentences, though the native speaker of American English falters badly at certain nouns.

It is not so bad as it seems, or sounds: to advance from a closed-mouth muteness to "I speak good coffee" is exciting, but it hardly resembles the language of Beckett or Nabokov. Still, it is language, after all, and one that pleases me by going on as it seems determined to, from strength to strength. And my jaw had not resumed its shape, still bulging outwards like a bit of Mars, and my passion for relief by water continued unabated.

I suppose that the weary expert, tracing his route from stroke to Broca's brain and back again, may avidly recite his best lines until he can stand them no more. I have no such troubles, reciting my best lines by heart almost as soon as having had them, because few of them there are. I would like to somehow purloin the best lines of my favorite authors, but that is not allowed: common sense forbids it, and I am left, at the very most, with a dozen lines of narrow prose and a million words of utterances in three languages, half of them making no sense at all.

If I did not have the median voice that speaks to me in more or less the idiom of everyday and the BBC man who fills in for me whenever I run into trouble, I would be left with three hours of exact talk, which is not very much. Not when you consider it in the round, but when you take it word by word, it amounts to quite a lot. And who's to say that three hours of discipline may not be all that one requires daily, and all the rest is silent frustration.

XXXV

Nothing beats another author for a touch of the world reseen as a touch of the void. The air outside was electric with the faint, shimmery vastness of mid-morning, and my heart was up. This was the first view I'd had of the outside world, minus the quarter of an hour I'd snatched earlier, in two or three months. Presumably the air toward noon would, like a dove descending, fill the sky with incandescent terror, by which time I would be safely home again among my books and other treasures.

But I am getting ahead of myself here. There were other things to do. For one thing, the house had to be safe, both outside and in; the walk by the pool had to be made even safer, and checks must be made that I would in no way injure myself with knives and water. There were other checks, too: principally it was a good thing that the house did not have a basement, where I might be supposed to injure myself, or a wealth of electrical appliances on which to mend my soul.

These things and others, not excluding the last visit from my phys ed champion, ended the recitation, and we were at last free to go down the hallway, down two or three steps, and so out of the vast, ever-receiving hallway that led to the outside world—still alive with sunlight and dazzle. I was out. Having just left behind me several books on an obscure shelf and a couple of prescriptions that I no longer had need for, I was the proud owner of a list of twelve, or rather six old and six new, including the delightful one called Ritalin, which is an amphetamine-like stimulant.

I revert to my brilliant colors of the morning, now full sunup in all his majesty and pomp. Fated to go no higher, perhaps, but doomed by some ironic quirk to seem to climb even higher in the arid sky. I vowed to keep my eyes on this infernal-glorious object, but I soon lost it in the fuss generated by having myself propelled from the wheelchair (in which all hospital journeys were taken).

A car roof intercepted my hypnotized gaze; a brilliant field of routine objects brought me in touch with the outside world again, from lapis lazuli that decked the flanks of the hospital proper to old-fashioned hayricks that dotted the field above. From old stone fences made to last the years to bright, screaming cars leaping past us at the intersections at an even seventy miles an hour. Such a world. And I had almost lost it.

I treated all this as a farewell to Broca and his boys, as if I were bidding farewell to a gang of ruffians at the gate, but of course I stood a very good chance of seeing him forever after, in one guise or another, for his influence was perdurable and bold. After all, he'd ripped half my skull down my face in a viscid quiver lasting only seconds, and he was not counting on being forgotten again. Nothing in all this stood a fair to medium chance of being overlooked, for old man Broca and his corrupt friends Foley and Chuzzlewit stood by, eager to perform again in the

teeth of my approximately slackened mouth and
my right ascending arm with two and a half fingers
retrieved, so far.

These calm events took me back to 1985,
when I had my first stroke, a paltry thing compared
to this, as I suggested earlier, with full restoration of
my left arm in three weeks and complete reduction
of the spell that seized my mouth in half an hour. A
pica, you might say, in comparison to this monster
of the solitudes. Yet who was counting strokes? If
you could have a second, a third might be waiting
for you in the wings, all bright and perky with new
dramas to play on your eroded skull. I had wondered
after the first stroke whether, in fact, there could
be another . . . and there was, almost toppling the
framework downward in its insensate plunge. And
would number three express itself as a whoosh of
pain from which you would not wake up?

Happily, I thought, I was going to prevail,
and my still defective mouth would come into its
own, not far down the track, even though my bouts
of protospeech did not extend very far and did
not happen very often. Still, my mouth continued
to slacken, and my impression of the whole
superstructure was that it was actually getting bigger
through growing outward, which seemed to promise
an Elephant Man who could eventually speak in his
impeded way.

The new house, which was in fact an
old house, made the eyes tingle with a lot of
splashy, vivid, quasi-electric effects. Hard to look

at, although I confess to being torn between the lachrymose delights of being home once again and the spellbound onset of the day. Even the blues and greens of the pool looked strident. The multicolored cushions hurt the eyes in the most amenable manner possible. The white of the peculiar skeletal framework of the struts and stays that surround the pool were truly dazzling and, out in the mainstream, the silver of the pool ladder was impossible to look at but was tolerated for the sheer electrical expenditure of its manners. The greens were assuredly dull in this context, but each time I looked at them I recovered a unique relationship with crocus and hibiscus that at first made my head swim but soon partitioned off in a neat division of greenery and flower to which I added an extra credit for flowering so heartily on my return.

The only drab member of this jazzy mélange was the slightly bamboo-patterned umbrella, which made an astonishing invisible gambit with its base and looked as if it were caught in a stationary fall. Down among the dead men it lisped its overture, and down among the live men it retained its station and staves.

Above everything towered the trees, some of them at weirdly contorted angles to the main body, some of them old and at least one hundred and fifty feet high, some of them no older than a year and blooming fit to beat the band. Since this was the back end of midsummer, the trees cast a spurious, dilapidated light, which at first revealed the morose side of their natures but with the varying shafts of sunlight suddenly burned an electric blue, for an instant dappling all other entrants with its tone.

I was amazed to watch, and they let me watch, for a period of half an hour at least. I had rediscovered an old land made new by suffering, but I caught myself when I realized that all through my various hospital experiences I had not even suffered a jot of pain. It had all been like a TV with the sound turned off and with nothing to respond to except the crazy caterwauling in my head, which stretched out, now and then, to an elaborate recovery system almost designed to please.

I had been through it, without being through with it. I had nothing to show for my two spells of memory loss: the first fake, and the second only too real. Both added up to naught, and I wish, somehow, they would liven up to give me, even at the cost of some gentle pain, what they were like. What I was asking for seemed like a stroke of lightning to me, and then another when all hell broke loose, and I returned from the intervening chamber a changed man, no longer able to count, add numbers, dial a telephone, and speak. So vast an amount of instantaneous change in a man merits some degree of apology, but I grew to understand that the apology was there in the matrix, slow to spring but eager to help, and would survive even the stroke in its determination to be counted.

I settled in to a peaceful routine almost at once, being willed by the bodies around me. I now go to bed at eleven o'clock at night, extended gradually to twelve thirty, and my habits have changed: for instance, I now eat the same dinner every night of mashed potatoes, turkey or ham, and richly marbled gravy. Once a week we go out to have a haddock and shrimp cocktail dinner, but this is the only fish I eat. I originally had lost fifty pounds, but on the suave advice of my advisers I now limit the loss to forty.

Each day my mouth relents its fatal grip on me, and some days I actually advance to phrase a word or two recognizable amid all the Calibanesque babble I trot out. I still am a very imperfect speaker, hoping to do better all the time but also hoping to strike some kind of bargain with the mouth so that, as it minimally restricts, day by day, I can keep pace with it, offering it my own little ever-swelling compromise. In this way I hope, once again, to have it both ways, either dealing with what I have been dealt or depending on generosity.

XXXVI

"What now, having come so far in your five-
month ordeal with stroke, are your main fears?" I
answer this semiofficiously, being stimulated by
the conversation but atrophied by the effort. All
things come to an end. Between these bewildering
alternatives I have a massive choice, beginning with
the ever-present fear that I will lose most of my hard-
earned language and pass again into the dark night
of the speechless. Closely accompanying such a
fate lies the fear that I will lose my legs or that I will
lose what little I have learned about the telephone.
The more you deal with dumbness, the more there
comes to light your misadventures, from believing
the telephone book operates by first names only to
believing you have all along been speaking fluent
English, whereas in fact all you say is gibberish.
These tragedies are closer than we think.

Finally reconciling myself to one fear only,
I zero in on a hobbyhorse of mine that has to do
with the misbehavior of ordinary words. Let me
exemplify: it's as if somebody else is guiding me to
a happy outcome but it's always wrong, as if some
of the right words cannot be said and others take
their places without mercy. I mean, to put it more
elaborately, when there's a word that has to be said
and another word blows it right out the window.
For instance, take the word *Plexiglas*, which I used
to have trouble with. Sometimes its image grows
ever larger, quite blotting out anything else I want

to say, to the extent that my speech is deformed in an unusual way, right up to and including all the possibilities of monomania. A kindred phenomenon occurs using the telephone, when all my best efforts at first writing down the number in a correct series of easy-to-read echelons, and my best efforts to transfer the numbers in the order prescribed, burn out and don't work.

What are these misfirings of the language we love? Whence do they come and cheat us of our true destiny? It's as if a malicious dragon enters the works from time to time and does his dirty deeds. I've often considered the contrary point of view, namely the possible advantage of having such a dragon, but there seem to be none unless, seeping through the dark ages of language, there are things that we do not understand.

You can tell that there is both a formal and an informal fear behind these shifts. The formal fear has to do with expectations of language and the informal has to do with the clatter when language goes off the rails and rapidly becomes an exercise in monkey chatter. I have not used the word *panic* as much as it has deserved, but who is to escape whipping when all our best language rests on a pinpoint and can be tipped over by the nearest blunder? Any departure from orthodox language may provoke either an absolute gibberish or a silence that listens to itself. You cannot always be on watch for the unseen, which erupts regularly in the thoroughfare of language. It appears like magma.

Hence all those long showers of gibberish, especially in my case around 5 p.m., when meaningful communication disappears into its own fundament and remains there until the next day. Some gifted speakers can actually make sense of these downers' diffidences, but they are rare and in demand. The sundowner soon learns that he is not getting through and watches television instead. Of all my discoveries in this field, I note the weighty growth of my language from muteness to near fluency in five months, a blessing that continues to amaze me. I still remember vividly, and always will, the phase when I emerged from the hospital and saw the apocalyptic lights of home once more. Unable to speak beyond a few words, I was an absolute duffer with all forms of language and print and totally incapable of facing the tasks invented by the speech therapists, such as "name an animal, a fruit, a season." Even now, at a near six-month distance, I still cannot improvise the word for hummingbird, and it occupies me still. I was impressed to have my knowledge of French restored to me unscathed. There is no understanding these mysteries, but one can be enormously grateful.

I have not spoken of the sudden irritability in the life of the stroke victim, which is very largely the result of pure frustration and might be presumed to improve as language improves. By the same token, these bouts of irritability have an impersonal bouquet, not aimed at anybody in particular but rather directed at the full panoply of language that has been denied. It is not irritability as much as a consuming desire to do better, and let's face it, not many people arrive again at the perfection they once knew. Caregivers are exhorted to receive the brunt of this, and they do most gracefully, bearing, most of them, a long-term memory of how it felt, at least as a proxy, to be deprived of all speech. My own outbursts of irritability or whatever you call it were frequent, and I would have been amazed if someone had recorded them so that I could hear them later.

Somewhere about the end of the first month of physical therapy, I realized for the first time what a kvetch and scold I had been, and I reduced my outbursts accordingly, transferring my objections to the loud sounds around me: air guns, buzz saws, and even knives rattling in a drawer. The universe sounded quite appreciably louder than it did before; this was also true of TV and the fearful noise of traffic. Were these shifts in response to a newly discovered vocalization of things or were they the rediscovery of an old status quo? This is a puzzle I leave for the ages. Similarly I am not sure why, but I am less interested in boxing, soccer, and cricket than I was, and I again ask: were these changes genuine novelties or were they the old games coming around again? I edge toward thinking them new because I view the natural world with a new zest and I swim with a far greater realization of what I'm doing. I love to sit for hours surveying the same scene even while contemplating some passages from the work of Delius or listening with spellbound accuracy to the agitated fumbling of some creature trying to get in from the outside.

An academic and medical committee's finding on my eventual fate was a sobering one: Diane asked these dozen if there was a chance that I could resume my writing, to which they all answered in the negative. When you have a blaze of golden light backing you up, even to the end, you delight in such opinions even though you regard them as fustian.

XXXVII

Four months later, my right hand, the one I write
with, makes a fairly good job of things. At least three-
fifths of it does, and it stays erect whenever I choose
to brandish it. Of the two misbehaving portions,
the cricket-injured one comes out a bit gnarled and
droopy, while the little finger still cannot reach the
thumbnail that daily I cant over it in hopes of finding
plunder. Maybe the pair of them will never come up
to snuff. As it is, the three enable me to write a fairly
good hand, snatching increasing visibility from the
lap of the literary gods. Four months ago the whole
right hand was useless and hung by my side; now
it is almost four-fifths of the genuine article and one
day will have a singular triumph of its own. One
woman worked daily on the little finger to make it
heal, pushing and pulling until it almost went numb,
with no effect. Another woman, an Indian, thought to
seduce it into compliance, but with the same result. I
massage it gently and wait.

A group of three women and one man have
crossed my path in the meantime: Josephine Miles,
who had a lame right arm, withered and defenseless,
the bounty of some childhood accident; Gretel
Ehrlich, whose title *A Match to the Heart*, instructs
us in the technique of being struck by lightning;
and Maxine Kumin, who had to wear a "halo" (a
sort of airframe) on her head for three months while
recovering from a bad accident. These women in their
various ways, exemplify the raw pluck and naked

resolve that get you through that kind of experience. The fourth person is Roy, the tiger tamer, who, apart from being mauled by his favorite, has had to learn to speak and walk all over again. I often wonder how these heroic figures languished, for a time at least, in the same state of unreadiness for life as I myself did while waiting to discover if I would ever speak again. I am persuaded these four, to whom I add a cast of thousands, must all in their various ways have put up with indescribable torments of the damned to get where they are going, and I feel each one has had to discover a new access of being to get anywhere at all. I salute them and wish them well in their repose.

My final bag of dreams includes the startling question of the speech therapist who inquired, "How many Indian tribes can you name?" I launched into "Iroquois, Sioux, Comanche, and Hopi," before giving up. There were scores more, but that was not too bad for a person who could not in the earlier stages name a single bird, flower, or wild animal. I have of late been introduced to a woman of seventy-three who almost does without dreaming. Since her stroke she has dreamed very little and has not missed it. Is this the end of the dreamland cantata, or is this the beginning of another dream condition about which we at present know nothing at all?

Compare my ignorance of the Hebrew when Diane brought back from New York a torah pointer with a miniature human hand attached to it, to make clean and easy reading of the sacred text. I promise to make good with its iron hand.